The Colorful World of Dogs

The Colorful World of Dogs

Cathay Books

John & Mary Holmes

Contents

This edition published, 1979 by
Cathay Books
59 Grosvenor Street,
London W1

© 1976 Hennerwood Publications Limited

ISBN 0 86178 026 4

Produced by Mandarin Publishers Limited
22A Westlands Road,
Quarry Bay, Hong Kong.

Printed in Hong Kong

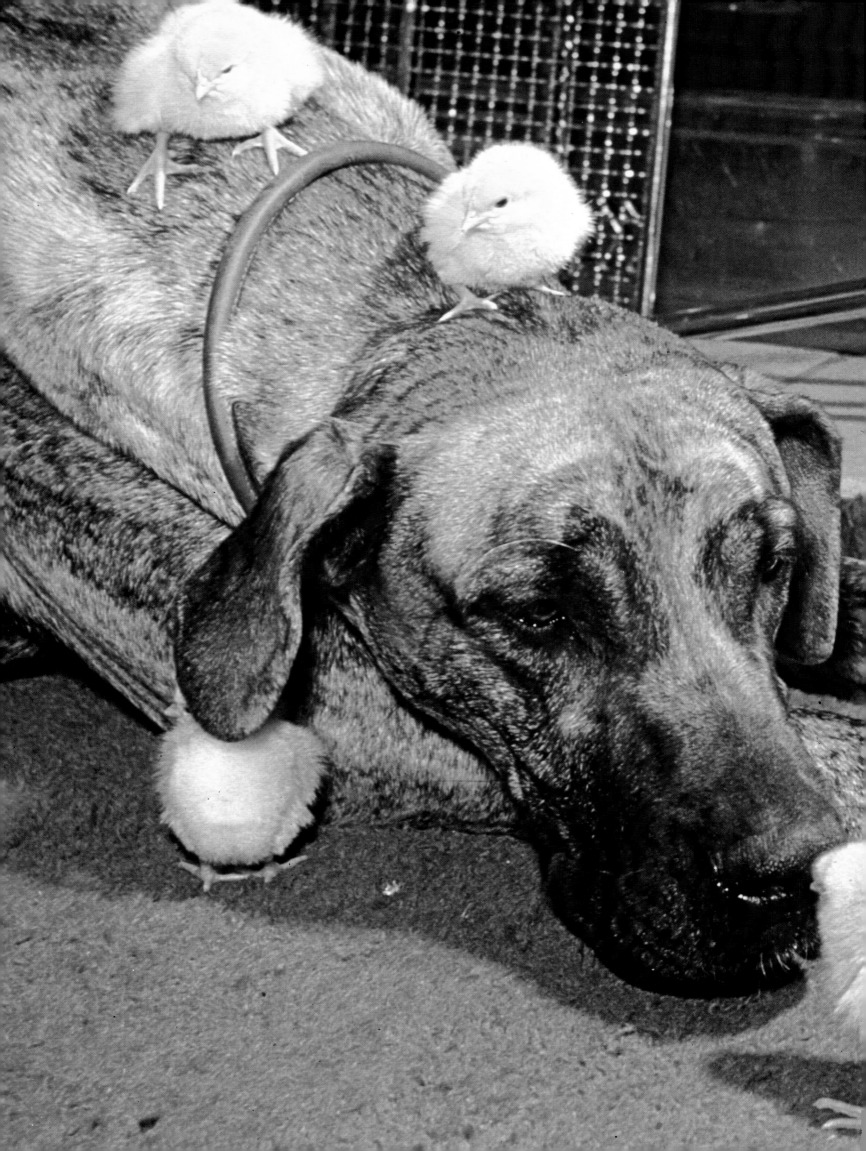

The Family Dog

Know Your Dog

IF asked what it is that has won the dog its unique position in its relationship with Man, the usual answer is that a dog is more intelligent and affectionate than other animals. But those who have worked with and studied other animals know this is not true. The cat, for instance, has just as much intelligence as a dog, but she uses it to her own ends, not her master's. She is also just as affectionate, but when she wants affection, not always when her master wants affection. Many wild animals taken from the nest at an early age and imprinted on a human foster mother are more affectionate and devoted than the average dog.

In fact, the dog has been such a wonderful servant and friend to Man because of its instincts, rather than its intelligence. This does not mean that dogs are not intelligent – far from it – but, contrary to common belief, intelligence does not make a dog trainable. Indeed, exceptional intelligence is the cause of many dogs being quite untrainable. Most difficult and disobedient dogs are very intelligent, and in some cases the whole problem arises from the fact that their intelligence surpasses that of their owners!

The first instinct to make itself apparent is the instinct for survival. Immediately it is born, the young puppy squirms about until it finds a teat and then sucks it. Intelligence or learning by association of ideas plays no part in this process; it is pure instinct that drives the puppy to find food.

Similarly, it is the maternal instinct which tells the bitch to clean up the foetal membrane and fluid and to stir the puppy into action by licking it. She does not have to be taught how to do it and she is unlikely to have seen another bitch doing it. Indeed, a maiden bitch is unlikely ever to have seen a newborn puppy before her own.

A dog's instincts vary enormously in strength between different breeds and individuals of the same breed. Again taking the maternal instinct as an example, we find that in some bitches it is so strong that they will happily adopt other puppies, kittens, lion cubs, piglets and other orphaned babies. On the other hand, some bitches which look after their own offspring very well will, if given the chance, kill newborn puppies belonging to another bitch, and some bitches are so devoid of maternal instinct that they simply walk off and leave their puppies to die. Intelligence has no connection with their behaviour, and it is surprising to observe how really 'stupid' an exceptionally intelligent bitch can be when it comes to looking after a family. Likewise, many bitches of low intelligence make most efficient mothers.

Most instincts provide pleasure to the dog, and consequently they grow stronger with usage. The maiden bitch will usually look with amazement at her first puppy, refusing to touch it for quite some time. As soon as she starts licking it she will become more and more enthusiastic, sometimes almost frantic, in her efforts to clean it. She will start licking her second puppy immediately, and when she has her next litter there will be no hesitation at all in cleaning the first puppy.

Another example of the dog's instinctive behaviour is a puppy retrieving a ball in response to the retrieving/hunting instinct with which we shall be dealing more fully later on. Many puppies will run after a ball and pick it up, sometimes bringing it back and sometimes running off to play with it. The first time it sees the ball 'running away', the puppy will usually lollop after it only half seriously. But if the game is continued, it will quickly become more and more enthusiastic until it can be relied on to fetch a ball every time it is thrown. This is one instinct which can grow stronger with usage to the extent of becoming overdeveloped and many dogs are completely obsessed by balls, sticks, stones or anything else they can carry.

There seems to be an age at which a dog's instincts tend to develop. A puppy which has shown no previous inclination to retrieve may suddenly decide to do so. If encouraged at this stage the instinct will quickly develop, but if discouraged it will weaken and possibly die out altogether. A dog which has never been allowed to play with a ball as a puppy is very unlikely to do so as an adult. Whether or not instincts flourish depends to a great extent on the strength of the instinct in the first place. Some dogs, particularly the gun dog breeds, have very strong retrieving instincts which will survive under very adverse conditions. At the opposite extreme, other dogs are so completely devoid of the retrieving instinct that it is impossible to persuade them to pick up anything at all. In between are the majority of dogs, which require training to develop the retrieving instinct or to keep it under control, as the case may be.

Instinct is something which is either there or not there. It can be strengthened, weakened or diverted, but it cannot be put there and it cannot be taken away. It may lie dormant throughout a dog's life, but once developed it can never be weakened again. A dog with an obsession for chasing balls may be controlled by training and by providing other outlets for its energy, but the basic obsession will always remain.

The canine instincts most important in a dog's relationship with Man are the pack instinct, the hunting instinct, the guarding instinct, the instinct to keep the nest clean, the sex instinct and the instinct of fear arising out of the instinct of self-preservation. Some of these will be dealt with in later chapters, but we will start here with the pack instinct. All animals have what is known as a 'pecking order', so called because it was first studied scientifically on poultry. A 'pecking order' simply means that in a flock of 26 animals,

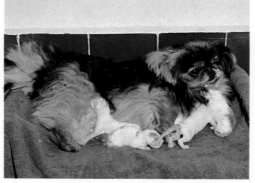

Above the strength of the maternal instinct varies enormously between individual bitches. Here a Pekingese which has lost her puppies is suckling a litter of Turkish Van kittens, which were four days old when the picture was taken.

Opposite: French shepherds with their dogs. Although the sheepdog's most important role is to herd and/or guard the flocks, most shepherds also value it as a faithful companion.

Right: Some bitches are very possessive about their puppies, especially in the early stages, but they are often pleased to show off their offspring to people they know and trust.

Below: Puppies normally enjoy playing together and get far more exercise this way than their owner is likely to provide. Care should be taken, however, to ensure that they do not become more attached to each other than to their owner.

Right: A dog chases and carries a ball in response to the hunting instinct. Chasing a ball gives your dog both an outlet for the instinct and at the same time plenty of physical exercise.

Below right: The herding instinct is only a slight deviation of the hunting instinct. In well-bred Border Collies the herding instinct is often strong enough to make the dog herd, or try to herd, literally anything that moves. Here the authors' bitch Queen is rounding up ducks in a lake!

A can peck anyone from B–Z, B pecks anyone from C–Z but not A, C pecks anyone from D – Z but not A or B, and so on until we come to poor Z who can peck no one but is pecked by everyone. In dogs it is not nearly so simple, although at first sight the principle is very similar. The pack leader does not simply dominate his subordinates, he actually keeps them all in order and tells them what to do. When the leader says 'Let's go hunting', they all go hunting; and when he says 'It's time to go home', they all go home. The majority of pack leaders are dogs, but a bitch can, and quite often does, take on the role.

Although every dog pack has a leader, the other members of the pack do not follow in a straightforward pecking order from A–Z. Often there are quite a number of dogs who neither dominate nor are dominated. Age also plays an important part and quite often one senior member of the pack will become more and more dominant until he attains the position of second-in-command; very often he will wait for an opportunity to overthrow the leader and take over that position for himself. If a pack leader dies without leaving a successor, there is considerable fighting and confusion for some time until a new leader emerges to take control.

Large packs of dogs are normally only found in the wild but, having kept quite a large and varied pack of domestic dogs for some thirty years, we have seen that this pack instinct is still very much alive.

Dogs are not 'almost human' and great suffering can be caused to them by people who think they are. But in some ways we are almost canine! Human and canine social habits have many similarities and it is this which enables Man to take over the role of pack leader. The dog's willingness to accept a human master as a substitute for a canine pack leader makes it easier to train than most other animals. Not only is it willing to be trained, it actually wants to be trained, and owners who neglect this can cause just as much suffering as those who starve their dogs.

The instinct of self-preservation which makes most wild dogs furtive and afraid of the unfamiliar is one of the instincts which is of little or no benefit to Man. It is from this instinct in the wild dog that nervousness in the domestic dog has evolved, and nervousness is the major cause of most dog problems. Nearly all cases of children being attacked by dogs and people being bitten by their own dogs arise from

nervousness; the dog is afraid it is going to be hurt and attacks first. In the evolution of the domestic dog, the instinct of self-preservation has been considerably weakened by simply breeding from bold dogs rather than nervous ones, but it has never been entirely removed.

Although essential if we are to continue breeding dogs, the sex instinct is another instinct which is of no benefit to Man and, under present-day conditions, is rarely of any benefit to the dog itself. Perhaps the saddest aspect of all this is that it is unnecessary, for the sex instinct is the only instinct which can be removed by a simple surgical operation: castrating the dog and spaying the bitch. The castrated dog is not only a happier dog, free from the worry and frustration of local bitches, it is also a much

nicer animal to have around. It will lose some of its pack leader instinct, which will only make it less likely to mark its territory by urinating on your furniture, less likely to fight other dogs and more submissive to the wishes of its human pack leader. We have not found that it alters any of the other instincts at all, and dogs guard, hunt, work sheep and retrieve game just as well after castration as before.

It is most important that dogs should be castrated after they have reached maturity, otherwise they lack character and initiative and become lazy, fat 'eunuchs'. The age at which a dog reaches sexual maturity varies enormously between individuals. Generally speaking, small breeds mature more quickly than large ones. The first clear indication is when the dog starts 'lifting its leg', which

may be as early as six months or as late as eighteen months. It is usually better to castrate too late than too early, and I have known dogs castrated at six or seven years old with no ill effects. It is better to leave a submissive dog until it is older, while a dominant one should be operated on much sooner.

Similarly, bitches should not be spayed until they have come in season at least once. Bitches spayed too early tend to be overweight and obese, which affects them mentally just as much as physically. Unlike castration, spaying done at the right time does not change a bitch's character at all. The owner who does not want to breed is saved a great deal of trouble and worry, and the bitch is spared the ordeal of being confined for three weeks twice a year. There is also some evidence to suggest that spayed bitches may be healthier, with less uterine disorders and no risk of false pregnancies.

The dog's various instincts can be strengthened or weakened by careful selective breeding. Through the ages Man has bred dogs to suit his own purposes, and in the process different breeds have evolved with their own characteristics. For many, but not all, of Man's purposes, the submissive aspect of the pack instinct is more important than the dominant aspect. We find breeds where the majority are submissive and willing to learn, while in others the majority are dominant and anxious to lead rather than be led.

A Greyhound chases a hare in response to the same instinct as a sheepdog works sheep. But as a result of selective breeding, various breeds of sheepdog have emerged where the majority are willing, even

anxious, to be trained. The same applies to gun dogs. With Greyhounds, Afghan Hounds and other hunting breeds the picture is a very different one. Once a hound has been unleashed to pursue its quarry, its master ceases to play any part. In many cases he simply follows it, so that in fact we have the dog leading and the master following. It is obvious that for this type of work a strong submissive instinct is not required, and hounds, and terriers too, are therefore generally much more difficult to train than gun dogs and sheepdogs. This is not due to lack of intelligence, and of course many hounds and terriers can be and are trained to be obedient, well-behaved animals.

Whether or not a dominant breed can be trained raises an aspect of the pack instinct which is often overlooked. It is easy for Man to take over as pack leader to his dog or dogs, but only if he is capable of leading. Nearly anyone can train a submissive dog, but a dominant dog can only be trained by a dominant person. Within a household, it is common to find a dog will obey some members of the family but not others. In recent years, trainers have tried more and more to study and practise the methods used by the canine pack leaders, with very successful results.

A good pack leader commands respect without bullying. He does not need to keep proving how big and strong he is, and therefore does not put himself in a position to be challenged. The most important lesson for the human owner to learn from the canine pack leader is that by gaining the respect of his subordinates he will also gain their affection and loyalty. The bully who

rules by force may obtain implicit obedience, but at the loss of friendship or affection.

Unfortunately a large number of trainers (including very successful trainers in trials and competitions of various types) adopt the latter policy. Never having trained by any other method, they have no idea of the pleasure they are losing in not having a dog which works *with* its master rather than *for* him – a dog which is a good servant *and* a loyal friend.

Above: These wolves are showing typical dominant and submissive attitudes. The submissive wolf exposes its throat to its dominant companion.

Right: Husky puppies in summer. This type of dog was developed to pull sledges in the Arctic, and in the past they were vital to the way of life of both the native Eskimo trappers and foreign explorers. Huskies were bred for the survival of the fittest and they will endure incredible conditions. At one time the Eskimos sometimes even cross-bred their Huskies with wolves. Although mechanical transport is gradually replacing the Huskies, they are still used in large numbers. Some are now kept as show dogs and companions, with varying degrees of success.

Overleaf: In many ways, Man has taken over the role of the pack leader.

Care and Grooming

THE dog has often been called 'Man's best friend' but, unfortunately, Man is not always the dog's best friend. A great number of pet dogs are either overfed, underfed, under-exercised, allowed to stray or kept in unsuitable conditions, and they suffer from various physical and mental disorders because their owners have not taken the trouble to find out more about the art of keeping a dog healthy and happy.

The dog was domesticated many thousands of years ago and, although it retains many of his natural instincts, it is now entirely dependent on Man for all its needs. So before deciding to take a dog into your home, think very carefully and make quite sure that you are willing and able to accept all the responsibilities that go with dog ownership. Small or large, the dog will need feeding, exercising, grooming, training and its health looked after. In case of illness your veterinary surgeon will be the person to consult, but any responsible owner should have some knowledge of first aid and know the symptoms of simple common ailments.

Feeding

Breeders often say that 'half the pedigree goes in at the mouth', and it is certainly true that the food a puppy is reared on will affect its whole future. Most adult dogs are adaptable animals and will usually eat a wide variety of foods, but any dog will be healthier and happier if fed a properly balanced diet. Dogs are by nature carnivores, that is to say meat-eaters, but today most are fed a mixed diet and appear to thrive on it. Our grandparents most likely fed their dogs on table scraps and left-overs, from which the dogs probably got sufficient nutrients, but today a lot of our food is processed, pasteurized, dehydrated, refrigerated, preserved and so on. If your dog is fed on scraps from these foods, its diet will very likely be short of a number of essential ingredients.

To keep in good health, your pet will therefore need proteins, carbohydrates, fats, minerals, vitamins and trace elements. Probably the simplest diet for your dog is meat and wholemeal biscuit meal, a diet which has been fed successfully to innumerable dogs for many years. But, as meat is so expensive, you may prefer to feed one of the many proprietary diets available. The pet food industry offers a

bewildering variety of diets for you to choose from. Most foods offered by the well-known firms contain all the essentials for your dog, but dogs, like people, are individuals and what suits one may not suit another. Some dogs like dry food, some like moist; some like tinned meat and some prefer raw meat. So if your dog does not like one type of food, try another, and don't forget that dogs like a change as much as we do. I can think of nothing more boring than being presented with the same food in the same dish at the same time every day. Proprietary foods are only as good as their contents and the care that goes into manufacturing them, so buy a reputable brand and if possible check on the label to see what the ingredients are.

Tinned dog food is usually cooked meat in various forms. Better-quality products have more meat than gravy, and as meat is

about 75% water, make sure you buy this type otherwise the poor dog is only having a meaty drink. If you find your dog prefers liver, chicken, rabbit or beef, let it have what it likes best. It makes very little difference what meat is in the tins, as most of the better-quality ones have vitamins and minerals added in the right proportions.

Another way of using meat, other than fresh, is dried meat. The good-quality product has a very high protein content and is very economical to feed. It must be well soaked in boiling water and allowed to cool before being mixed with wholemeal biscuit to make a balanced meal.

So-called 'soft-moist' foods are popular with many dogs. Usually bought in plastic bags, these are meaty foods which some dogs prefer to dry ones. The product keeps very well until opened but must then be used up fairly quickly.

One very dry type of food is called extruded or expanded. This is cooked under less heat than biscuit and has a very high food value. It looks like a rusk or very light biscuit meal and forms a complete diet on its own. If you are changing your dog to this type of food from a more conventional diet, do so gradually as it will need time to adjust to the change. Other dry foods are the pelleted and flaked diets, which are also complete feeds. The flaked diet has the same contents as the pellets, and has the advantage that it can be fed moist if the dog prefers. On the other hand, the manufacturers claim that the pellet form is more easily digested. It can be bought in large or small pellets, depending on the size of the dog.

When feeding any of these dry diets, it is essential that the dog should be supplied with water all the time. If you remember that meat contains about 75% water and these dried foods only have a water content of about 8%, you can see that the success of feeding them depends very much on water being available as required.

One meal a day is usually enough for most dogs, but if for some reason you prefer to split this and feed two smaller meals, it will do no harm. In fact, in some cases it is a good thing. Very small dogs, giant breeds and old dogs are probably better fed twice a day. This ensures that the stomach is not overloaded and makes digestion easier. It is almost impossible to advise people what amount of food to give their own pet dog. Like people, some dogs are good converters of food and some are bad, and, like people, most dogs are overweight. An active, high-spirited dog will eat far more than a stolid, lazy dog of the same size. It is easier to put weight on a dog than take it off, so if your dog has a tendency to get fat feed him a little less.

It is much better not to give dogs titbits. It only makes them bad-mannered, always begging for food, and upsets their stomachs. Special dog chocolate drops and other candy do no harm if they are given in moderation, as an aid to training or for some special reward. Dogs do not need bones in their diet, but if you want to give your pet a bone to gnaw make sure it is a large raw marrow bone. Cooked bones, especially poultry and chop bones, are very dangerous. The cooking makes the bones brittle and they can splinter and pierce the intestines, often with disastrous results. Hard nylon 'bones' or raw hide strips are good for dogs to chew and help to keep their teeth clean, or you could give a large, hard dog biscuit for the same purpose.

When you feed your dog does not matter, but do not give it a heavy meal and then take it out for a run. If you can steel yourself to do it, all dogs benefit from a 'fast day' once a week. It gives the dog's stomach a rest, and if yours is a fussy feeder it does help considerably in getting a clean plate.

Equipment

It is quite possible to buy your dog almost as large a wardrobe as your own. There are plastic raincoats, tweed winter coats, woolly football jerseys, leggings, rainhats, dainty beds with foam mattresses, and so on, but your dog will not thank you for, nor will it need, all these expensive luxury items.

There are certain essential items that

Left: Dogs enjoy chewing bones and it is good for their teeth. Large bones are best. They should never be cooked, as cooked chicken, rabbit or mutton bones can break into very dangerous splinters.

Below: Your dog's food and water bowls should be kept just as clean as the plates you use yourself.

Opposite: A young St Bernard on a long nylon lead, of the type often used in the show ring.

Right: Swimming is excellent exercise for dogs and makes an enjoyable change, especially in hot weather. Never try to teach a dog to swim by throwing it into the water. Many dogs have been very effectively put off water for life by this approach.

Below left: A tennis racquet can send a ball much farther than if you throw it by hand. Apart from exercising the dog, this game can and should be used to teach obedience. The dog should not move until told to do so, and it should bring the ball straight back and deliver it to your hand.

all dogs do need, however. Every dog needs a collar and lead. Collars can be the ordinary flat leather buckled type, narrow round ones, studded leather collars and, of course, fancy studded collars for poodles. You can also buy collars in nylon, which is very strong and durable, not to mention washable, and it is very light for the dog to wear. Chain collars are usually 'slip collars' and are often used for training. Slip collars should never be left on a dog, as the ring can easily get caught up in something like a car door handle and the dog could be strangled. They should be kept strictly for training. From the dog's point of view, a light collar is best and it is preferable to take the collar off at night. Your name and address will need to be fixed to the collar. This can be engraved on a plate or disc, or written on a slip of paper and put in a small barrel attached to the collar. The latter method is the most useful as you can change the address if you take the dog on holiday with you.

Leads are available in any of the materials already mentioned for collars. Chain leads are not very practical, unless the dog eats leather ones. Leather leads are ideal if they are made of good-quality leather and are kept supple. Nylon is very strong and has the advantage that it can be rolled up and put in your pocket. All leads should be a reasonable length (short leads encourage a dog to pull), with strong clips.

Your dog will also need its own food and water bowls. These are obtainable in a variety of shapes and sizes, usually in plastic, aluminium, stainless steel or earthenware. Make sure they are easy to clean. If you have a dog, like a spaniel, which has long ears, get one of the bowls specially styled for these dogs. They are much narrower at the top, and the dog will not get its ears in a mess when eating.

You will also need to give your dog its own bed. There are plenty of styles to choose from, but basically the bed needs to be raised off the floor to keep it out of draughts, easy to clean and comfortable. Although a lot of dogs sleep curled up, a bed should be large enough for it to sleep stretched out if it wants to. Baskets are not advisable as they tend to harbour dirt and fleas. A folded-up blanket or piece of carpet can be placed in the bed. This should be washable, and to keep it clean longer you can put a 'dog sheet' over it, either buttoned or zipped on. There are also heated dog beds on the market. Normally these are not necessary, but with old or sick dogs they

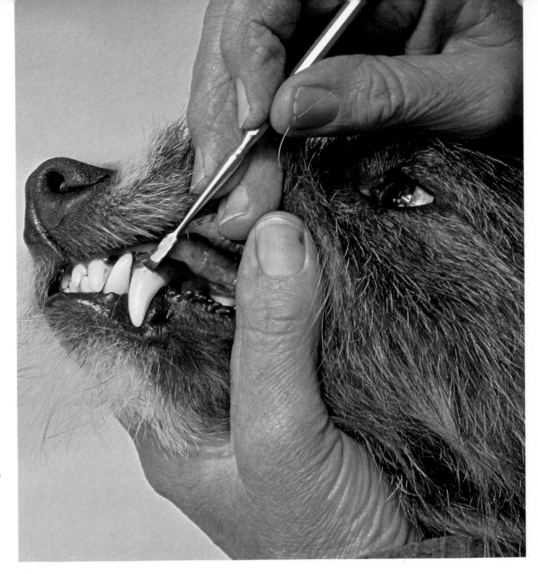

Right: Scaling teeth. If you have a firm, steady hand and dog which you can control this task is not difficult, but if you are hesitant to do it yourself you may prefer to visit a veterinary surgeon or dog's 'beauty parlour'.

Far right: Using a hound glove on a smooth-coated dog. You should exert plenty of pressure, which will tone up the dog's muscles as well as groom its coat.

can be very useful. Small dogs are often best kept in a small indoor kennel. It gives them a feeling of security and keeps them warm and cosy. The kennel can also be used as a travelling box.

Some grooming equipment will be necessary. All breeds need a brush and comb, nail clippers, a pair of scissors, a tooth scaler if you wish to look after the dog's teeth yourself, a rough towel and a chamois leather for drying. A hairdryer is useful for the longer-coated breeds as it is difficult to get their coats looking good if they are only rubbed with a towel. Short-coated breeds will need a hound glove or mitt instead of a comb. These are often made of rubber or double-sided, one side with very short wire pins or bristles and the other covered in some material, such as velveteen, to give the coat a final polish. Nail clippers can be bought in the shape of pliers or what is known as the 'guillotine' type. Most dogs seem to prefer the latter. A coarse steel nail file is also useful to finish off the rough edges on the nails. It is no good going to a lot of trouble grooming your dog if you are using a dirty brush and comb, so make sure these are washable and give them a wash at least once a week.

A great number of dogs are seen wearing coats, but very few actually need to. It may please the owner to put his pet into a pretty coloured jersey but the dog will probably be happier and healthier without it. Some of the very small, thin-coated breeds do feel the cold, however, and on wet windy days they may be better off with a little extra protection, and of course coats are a help if the dog is sick or has a touch of rheumatism.

Exercise

All dogs, small or large, need exercise, and most need far more exercise than they are given. They all need at least thirty minutes free running exercise daily, more if possible. Left to their own devices, very few dogs will take much exercise, so to exercise your dog properly you will have to exercise yourself. It will probably do you as much good as the dog!

Small dogs can get a lot of exercise in a confined space, but they will still appreciate a change and the chance to romp in the open. If you teach your dog to retrieve (most dogs learn quite readily), it can be a great help in exercising it. If time is short and you cannot get to a park or take it for a walk in the country, you can still give it a lot of exercise in a small garden. Hide various objects or its favourite ball and then send it to look for them, or use a tennis racquet and a couple of balls and bat the balls out in different directions, then send the dog for them one at a time. Dogs can get very keen on this 'game' and, apart from physical exercise, it teaches a dog control, concentration and gives it a chance to use its nose.

Another sport enjoyed by many dogs, especially gun dog breeds, is swimming. If a young dog is reluctant to go into the water, never force it or, worse still, throw it in. Encourage it by throwing a ball into the water, going in yourself, or having another dog that likes swimming to go in first. Choose a warm day and a calm lake or river with a gradually sloping bank. Swimming is excellent exercise and a short swim will do your dog as much good as a much longer period of running.

Some of the larger, active breeds, such as Dobermans and German Shepherds, enjoy running beside a bicycle, but don't overdo it and don't go too fast. And only let a dog run beside a bicycle on traffic-free roads.

You will probably find other activities for your dog to enjoy and the more varied exercise you can give it, the more it will benefit. On cold, wet days even small dogs will be all right if kept moving, but don't leave them to stand about doing nothing, and always dry a wet dog on return to the house. In very hot weather, exercise, except swimming, should be carried out in early morning or late evening when it is coolest, as dogs can suffer quite badly from heat stroke.

Grooming

Grooming should not be looked on as a chore, or a battle. Both you and your dog should enjoy it. Grooming is necessary for all dogs, short- or long-coated. It keeps the dog clean and tidy, tones up the skin and muscles, gets rid of loose hair and encourages the new coat to grow through more rapidly.

The first essentials for a happy, easy grooming session are the right sort of brushes and combs and a dog that has been trained to lie down and keep still while you groom it. Most sensible dogs, groomed regularly and correctly, enjoy the procedure. In fact, it should strengthen the bond between dog and owner. In a pack of wild dogs, 'social grooming' takes place between individuals, and is one of the ways in which wild dogs show affection towards one another.

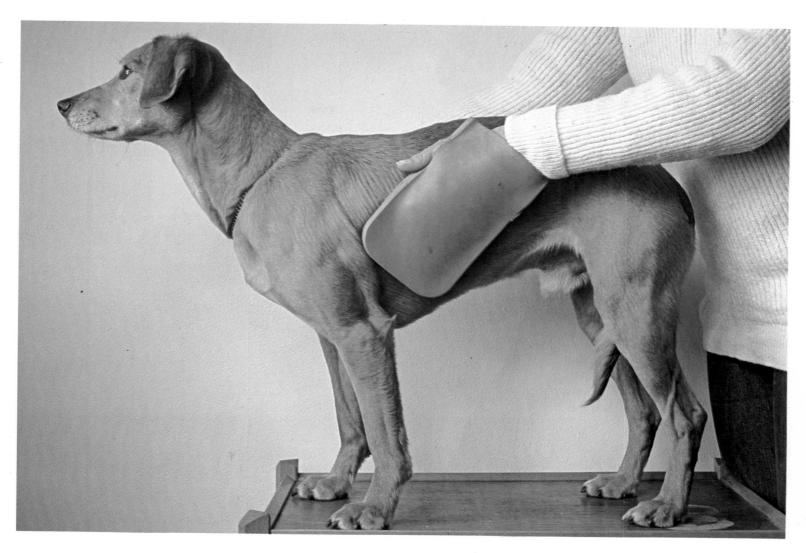

It is best to give the dog a few minutes grooming daily and a thorough groom once a week. Take the opportunity to give it a good check-over at the same time as the weekly grooming session. Starting at the head, open the mouth and check the teeth and gums. If the teeth show signs of tartar deposit, you can remove it yourself with a tooth scaler. The teeth must be scaled from the gums to the tip of the tooth. This is fairly simple to do if there is only a light deposit of tartar, but, if possible, it is advisable to be shown how to do it correctly. Heavy tartar causes receding gums, bad breath and decaying teeth, so if the teeth have been allowed to become heavily encrusted consult your veterinary surgeon. When you are doing the weekly grooming, you can clean the teeth with an ordinary toothbrush which helps to keep the deposits down.

Next check the eyes. These should be bright and clear, and any discharge should be checked with your veterinary surgeon. Some breeds with protruding eyes or very deep-set ones seem to accumulate dirt and dust in the corners, causing irritation and often making the eyes water. One of the best and cheapest eye solutions is the normal saline solution. Just mix 1 teaspoonful of salt into ½ litre (1 pint) of boiled water and allow it to cool.

While you are looking at the dog's head, you should also check the ears. Dogs with longish, hairy ears, such as spaniels and poodles, pick up all sorts of things on their ear flaps, which can mat the hair and cause discomfort. Have a look inside the ear, and if the inside of the ear flap is rather grubby, wipe it round with a piece of damp cottonwool. Never poke or probe into the ear itself; you cannot see down the ear without a proper instrument and if there is any obstruction you could easily push it down even further. If there is no discharge and the ear smells fresh but it seems to irritate the dog, try pouring a little warm olive oil down it. This should soothe the ear and if there is a bit of dirt inside it will help to float it out. Apart from this simple treatment, never mess about with ear troubles, but take the dog to the veterinary surgeon.

Some dogs get cracked noses in very dry or very cold weather. A little oil rubbed in usually relieves this trouble.

Make sure the feet have no cut pads, thorns, cysts between the toes, or mats of hair. Some city dogs get cracked pads from too much walking on concrete. A little oil will often help and the dog can wear special boots for a few days until the pads heal. If there are mats of hair under the pads or between the toes, cut these out very carefully with a pair of sharp, blunt-ended, curved scissors. If these mats are left, they accumulate dirt and set up an irritation which can lead to eczema. This will need professional treatment.

Keep the nails short and do not forget the dew claws. These are small extra claws found on the inside of the feet, rather like a thumb in humans. They are usually in the forefeet only, but some breeds also have hind dew claws. As these claws do not reach the ground, they are not worn down and will need regular clipping. If not attended to frequently, they can grow right round into the foot and cause a nasty abscess. You may be lucky and own a breed in which the dew claws have been removed.

Use a nail clipper and file to keep the dog's nails in trim. The nails have a sensitive 'quick' running down the centre; in a white nail this shows up as a pink streak. Care should be taken to avoid cutting this, as not only is it painful for the dog, it also bleeds profusely. If you just cut the pointed tip of the nail, it should be safe even if the dog has black nails where you cannot see the tip. After you have clipped the nails, finish them off with a coarse file, drawing down from the root of the nail to the tip. If you file the nails regularly, the quick recedes and you will not need to use the clippers so frequently.

Under the dog's tail are two small glands, called the anal glands, situated on either side of the anus. The wild dog does not just eat meat, it eats the skin and bones as well, and this helps to keep the anal glands emptied, but because the domestic dog has less roughage in its diet, these glands fill up and do not empty of their own accord. A very evil-smelling liquid collects and can cause an abscess if it is not removed. The glands can be emptied quite easily by holding a pad of cottonwool over them and squeezing firmly on either side. Although a simple job when you know how, it is a good idea to ask your veterinary surgeon to show you the first time.

Now we come to the coat itself. In a short-coated dog it takes very little time or trouble to keep the coat in good clean condition, but short-coated dogs do tend to shed their coat a lot. This is partly because most dogs are kept in centrally heated houses with artificial 'daylight', so they do not shed naturally with the seasons. A good brushing with a stiff bristled brush, hound glove or mitt and a final polish with your own hands should be enough. A rubber hound glove is very useful to help out the dead coat. With a long-coated breed you will need a different technique. You need a good stiff brush with longer bristles and a comb with wide teeth. The comb should be used as little as possible so that the coat is not pulled out unnecessarily. Start at the rear end and vigorously brush out the coat, a little at a time until you reach the head. Then go back over the whole dog again. Comb out the feathering on the ears, tail and legs, but do it very carefully. Tease out any small mats of hair with your fingers.

Terriers need special treatment. Unless they are of the smooth variety, such as the Smooth Fox Terrier, they will require regular 'stripping'. Terriers should have a soft thick undercoat and a harsh top coat. When the dog needs stripping the outer, hard coat is pulled out with a stripping knife. This is usually a sort of penknife with serrated edges, but there are a number of different types. All terriers are stripped to a different pattern, according to their breed. It is not that difficult to do it yourself, but try to get a breeder to show you how. For daily grooming, the terrier just needs the usual check-over and a good brushing with a stiff brush.

Dogs with thick, stand-off coats like Pomeranians, Keeshonds and Samoyeds need to have their coats brushed up the wrong way first and then carefully brushed back into place. Poodles, which incidentally do not shed their coats like other breeds, need to be clipped. If you want some of the fancy clips you will need to take the dog to

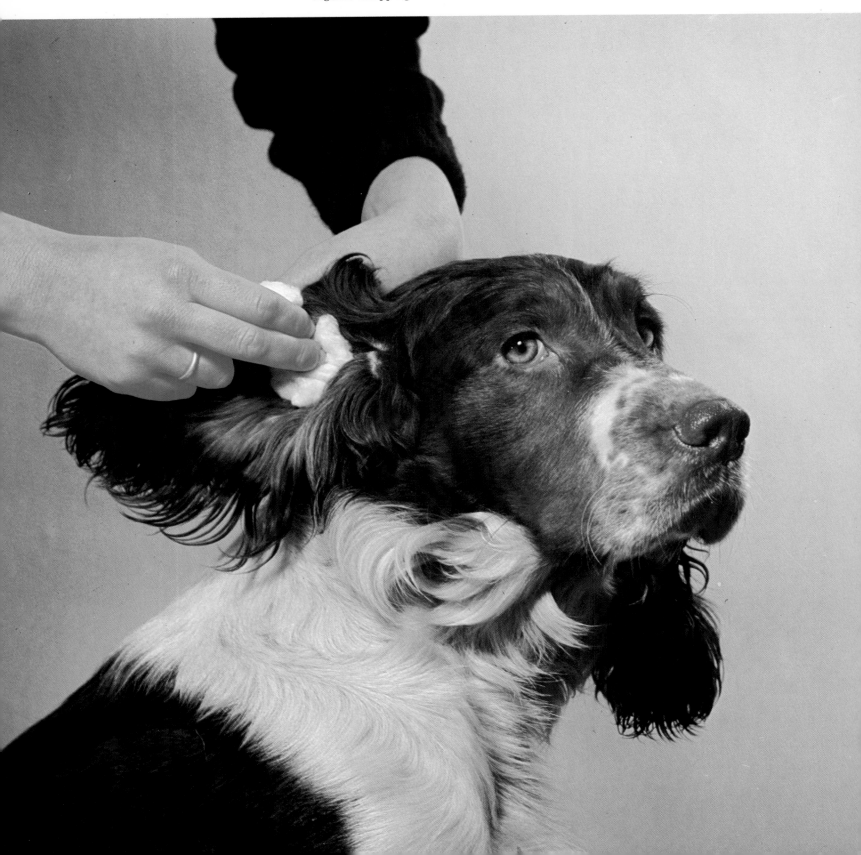

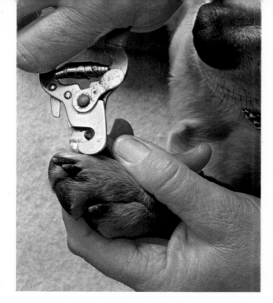

a beauty parlour, but for a simple lamb clip you can learn to do it yourself. You will need either electric or hand clippers and a pair of sharp hairdressing scissors. If you can get some instruction, so much the better, but failing that there are a number of specialist books on the market which will show you how to do the job. Do not forget to keep your grooming equipment clean; there is no point brushing a dog with a dirty brush.

When your dog is dirty it will need a bath. How often you bath it will depend on the weather and how dirty it gets. Pour some warm water into a suitable container, either sink, bowl or bath, stand the dog in the water, pour on some shampoo and work up a good lather. Leave the dog's head to last; once it is wet, the dog will try to shake. Give the rest of the dog a good

washing, and rinse it very well – at least twice in tepid water. Finally wash the head, being careful not to get shampoo into the eyes or to get the inside of the ears wet. If you are outdoors, let the dog out, on a leash, and once it has given a good shake rub it dry with a large rough towel. Indoors, it is best if you put the towel right over the dog to remove the surplus moisture. In either case, an electric hairdryer is ideal for drying the dog off completely, especially for long-haired breeds; brush and comb the coat as you dry it, otherwise it will dry into a tangled mass. If it is a warm sunny day, the dog can run about outside to dry itself, but take care that it does not try to roll on the ground and undo all your good work. Make sure you keep it busy playing, say with a ball, or be sure the surface of the ground is clean and dry.

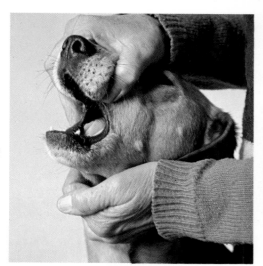

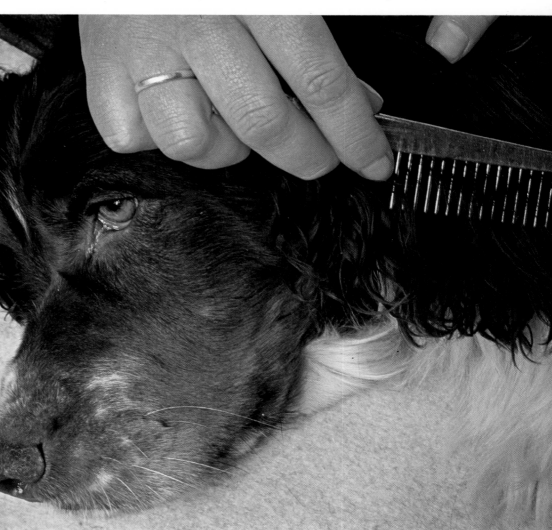

Opposite: Cleaning a spaniel's ears.

Top left: Nail-clipping, using 'guillotine' clippers.

Middle left: Dogs with feathering, such as spaniels and setters, are better brushed with a stiff brush. If they are very muddy, however, it is easier and quicker to use a comb. Provided this is only done occasionally, and a wide-toothed comb is used, no harm will be done.

Bottom left: Opening the dog's mouth, so that you can give it a pill or remove a bone or any other object which is causing it distress. Gently press its lips over its top teeth, which will make it open its mouth. If you are doing this for the first time, you may need to use both hands and have someone else to help you.

Above: Combing the ears. The comb should be moved from the skin outwards.

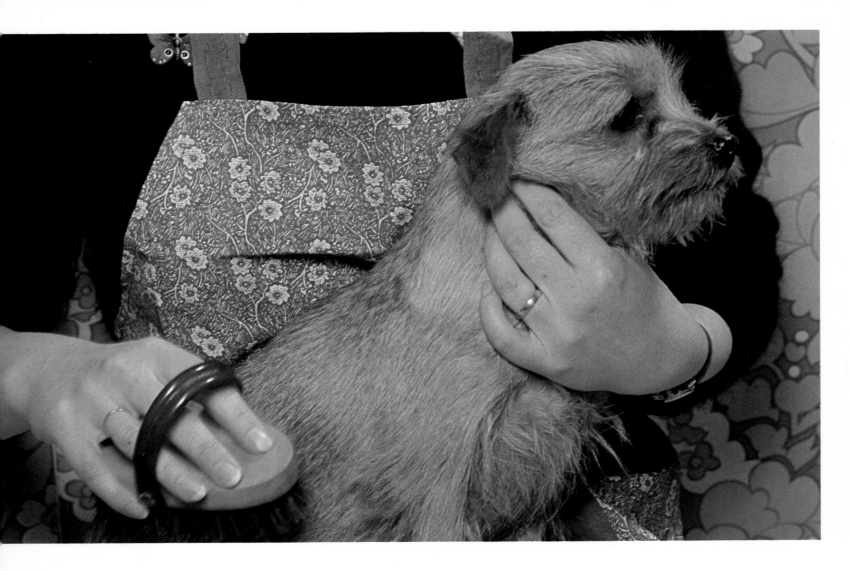

Above: Brushing a small, wire-coated dog. You can also stand the dog up on a table so that you can exert more pressure on the brush. This also teaches show dogs to stand up to be handled by the judge.

Opposite: Children should always be encouraged to groom their own dogs. Here we have an excellent example of a happy child/puppy relationship.

One very good way of freeing a dog from fleas, lice or other unwanted guests is to give it a medicated bath. Most pet stores have a good selection, and if you follow the instructions carefully they are usually most effective. Remember, though, that fleas do not breed on the dog but in its bedding or in cracks in the floorboards, so it is no use bathing the dog without also washing its bed, the bedding and the immediate surroundings.

There are other methods of getting rid of fleas, besides bathing the dog. 'Flea collars' are very effective. They are specially impregnated plastic collars which last up to about three months and really do seem to keep the dog free from fleas. Alternatively, there are aerosols which can be sprayed into the dog's coat. Be careful when you are using these to keep them pointed away from the dog's face. The coat can also be turned back and insect powders shaken onto the exposed skin.

Unfortunately, however well cared for your dog is, it is almost certain that it will pick up a few fleas from time to time, so when grooming it always check to see that there are no fleas or traces of flea dirt (little black specks) in the coat. If they are not discovered fairly quickly, fleas set up intense irritation which makes the dog scratch, and this in turn can lead to skin troubles which are much more difficult to cure than the odd flea.

General health care
There are one or two simple things you should learn to do to help the dog yourself before you need to call in a veterinary

surgeon. The first is being able to take a dog's temperature. The normal temperature should be about 38.61°C (101.5°F) and anything over two degrees of fever should be regarded as a warning of something serious. The temperature should be taken in the rectum. Grease the end of a *snub-nosed* thermometer and insert it gently into the dog's rectum. Hold it there for the required time and then gently remove it. Do not let go of the thermometer once it is inserted, as it has been known for dogs to pull them right inside!

Next you need to know how to give medicine to the dog. If this is liquid, you will find it easier to put it in a small bottle rather than trying to tip it out of a spoon. Have the dog sitting and if possible have someone holding it steady. Insert a finger between the dog's lips on one side of the mouth, pull them slightly apart and outwards and you will find that this forms a most convenient 'pocket' into which you can carefully pour the liquid. Keep its head slightly back and only pour in a small quantity at a time which it can swallow easily. Continue slowly until you have poured in the whole dose. Keep the dog's mouth shut and gently massage its throat to make sure that it has swallowed all the medicine.

You may also need to give your dog a pill or capsule. Some people try to put it in its food, but this is inadvisable as the dog might spit it out in pieces, eat half of it or it may be the sort of medicine that should not be given with food. The best way is to place your hand over the dog's face and on either side press its lips over its top teeth;

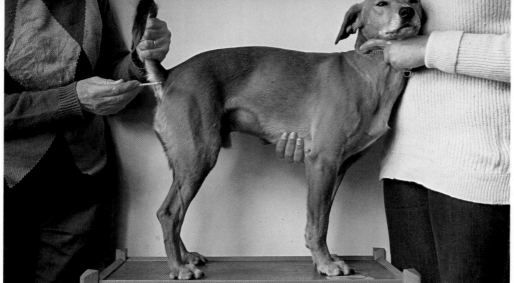

Left: Taking the dog's temperature. Hold the dog firmly and gently insert a blunt-nosed thermometer.

Left below: An emergency muzzle can be made from a length of bandage or any long piece of material. This is the belt of a dressing gown.

Below: Administering liquid medicine. Pull out the dog's cheek to form a pouch into which to pour the liquid.

Bottom: Dogs, like people, are more pleasant to live with if they have a bath when necessary.

Right: A hairdryer can be a great help with long-coated breeds, especially if the weather is bad.

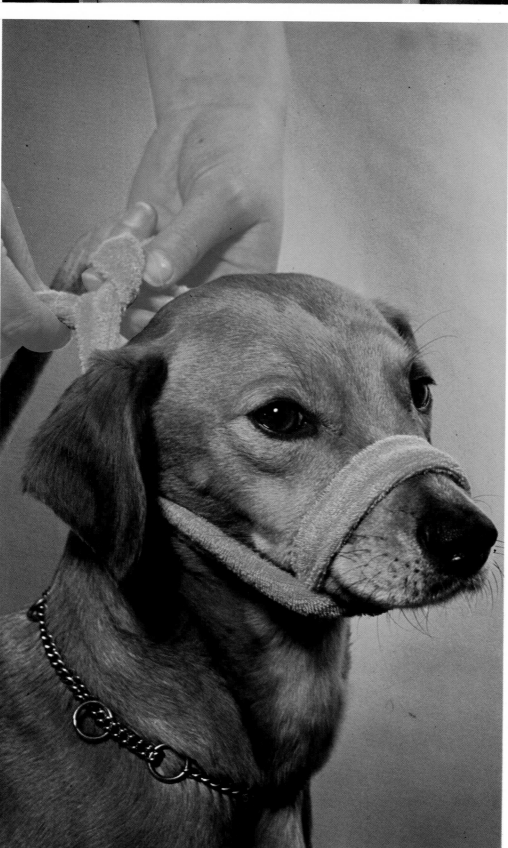

this will make it open its mouth. Tip its head slightly backwards, and with your other hand drop the capsule right at the back of the tongue. Withdraw your hand quickly, shut the dog's mouth and watch for it to swallow. If it appears to be holding the pill in its mouth, massage its throat gently or close its nostrils for a few seconds.

Something else every owner should know how to do is put an emergency muzzle on a dog. Any dog involved in an accident, in pain and frightened, is liable to bite in fear and it is only common sense to protect yourself. A large handkerchief, soft belt, tie, scarf or odd strip of cloth can all be used. Make a loop, slip it over the dog's nose and pull the knot tight under its chin; take both ends back and tie them firmly behind its ears. You should then be able to handle the dog safely.

By now you should know what a healthy dog looks like, your own dog in particular, so any signs of abnormality should be carefully watched. Look for dull

eyes instead of bright ones, an active dog that suddenly refuses to go for a walk, a placid dog which becomes irritable, excessive thirst, lack of appetite in a normally greedy dog, excessive scratching, especially round the ears, or the dog holding its head to one side. These are just a few of the more obvious signs that all is not well.

The veterinary surgeon should always be consulted sooner rather than later, but there are a few things that require his immediate attention. Very severe vomiting should never be allowed to continue for more than an hour or two at the most. Give the dog nothing at all by mouth and take it straight to the vet. Diarrhoea is often due to a change of food or a stomach upset of some sort and will often clear up quickly by itself, but if it continues for more than 24 hours the dog should be seen by the vet. In all cases where you suspect the dog is not well and the symptoms do not clear up quickly, do get in touch with your veterinary surgeon. A large number of illnesses if treated promptly cause little harm, but if left to get a good hold can be very serious indeed.

First Aid

Accidents. Traffic accidents are probably the most common accidents suffered by dogs. Move the dog as little as possible, as it is most likely suffering from shock and possibly internal injuries. If there is excessive bleeding, it must be stopped. First check that there is nothing in the wound, then apply a pad of gauze if any is available (if not, use a clean handkerchief, torn sheet or the most suitable clean covering you can find). Then bandage firmly over the pad. If blood seeps through, rebandage on top and take the dog to the vet immediately. To move a large injured dog with as little disturbance as possible, it is best to use a blanket. Slide it gently under the dog and, with one person at each end holding two corners, gently lift the dog into a car.

If the dog is suffering from internal bleeding, its breathing will be rapid and shallow, its skin will feel clammy, its pulse will be rapid and it may be unconscious. In this case, simply get it to the veterinary surgeon just as fast as you can.

Burns. Extensive burns are very dangerous. The only recommended first aid is to immerse the part in cold water and get professional treatment immediately.

Heat stroke. In very hot weather or if it is left in a closed car, even in warm weather, dogs can suffer badly from heat stroke. The dog will probably be panting, weak and near to collapse. It might be vomiting, and its temperature will be very high. Lower the temperature as soon as you can – if you are indoors immerse the dog in a cold bath; outdoors you may be able to find a hose, or failing that a tap, where you can get water to pour over it. Once the dog shows signs of recovery, dry it off, keep it in a cool place and encourage it to drink.

Poisoning. If you know the dog has taken poison, try to make it vomit. A small piece of washing soda pushed down its throat, or salt and mustard in water, will usually work quickly. Take the dog to the veterinary surgeon at once, and if you know what it has swallowed take along the packet or bottle.

Drowning. Contrary to general belief, not all dogs can swim. Even a dog that is normally a good swimmer may fall off a bridge and hurt itself, or get trapped in a steep-sided pond where it is unable to get out. The first thing to do is to place the dog's head lower than its body, pull out its tongue, try to drain out any excess water from its mouth and apply artificial respiration. Place the dog on its right side, tongue out and head forward, put your hand over its ribs behind the shoulder blade, press down on the ribs and release the pressure immediately. Repeat at intervals of about five seconds with short, sharp movements until the dog starts breathing normally.

Choking. Small rubber balls are the most usual cause of choking in dogs. The dog will be in considerable distress and, although able to breathe, will be unable to swallow and will salivate profusely. You will probably be able to feel the ball in its throat. The dog should be seen as soon as possible by a veterinary surgeon, who may have to anaesthetize it before removing the object.

Dogs sometimes also get a rubber ball stuck behind their molar teeth, causing an obstruction. If possible try to remove the ball, but be careful not to push it further down. Bones, pieces of stick and even stones can equally become lodged in the back of the mouth and cause a nasty wound. A dog with something wedged in its mouth usually paws frantically at its mouth or rubs it along the ground, slobbering profusely. Open its mouth carefully, taking care not to get bitten, and see if you can pull out the offending object. If you cannot get hold of it take the dog to the veterinary surgeon, who will give it an anaesthetic before removing the object and treating the wound.

Prevention is better than cure so try to keep your dog away from poisons, cooking stoves, unguarded fires, needles and sharp bones. Do not let it run loose on the streets, and never leave it shut in a closed car. And if it should be unlucky and suffer an accident, apply suitable first aid and then get it treated by the veterinary surgeon as soon as possible.

Above left: Picking up an injured dog on a blanket.

Right: A visit to the vet need not be an ordeal for the dog if it learns that it is being helped and is among friends. This Boxer is being gently held and comforted while its injured paw is bandaged.

All About Puppies

DOG breeders sometimes maintain that all problem dogs are made that way by their owners. This is often only an excuse for the unsuitable or untrainable puppies they have sold. We believe that the finished article depends about 50% on inherited characteristics and 50% on acquired ones. As you hope that the animal you are about to buy will be a member of the family for the next ten to fifteen years, it is worth going to a great deal of trouble in choosing it.

Once you have decided on which breed to have, you should try to find a seven- to eight-week-old puppy of that breed. Temperament is by far the most important factor in choosing a puppy. In dogs a good temperament is one that is bold, friendly and not afraid of noise or people; a bad temperament is one that is shy or nervous in any way. The majority of puppies may appear to have good temperaments, but only a minority end up as bold, friendly dogs. In choosing a puppy, its own behaviour is less important than the behaviour of its parents, grandparents and even great grandparents. It is unlikely that you will be able to see all those, but do try to see the parents and as many relatives as possible. If they are not the sort of dog you would like to own, try somewhere else. You should pay particular attention to the temperament of the dam. Geneticists believe that an animal inherits its various characteristics 50/50 from sire and dam, but by the time it is weaned a puppy will also have acquired other characteristics from its mother, or foster mother as the case may be. Experiments have been carried out where puppies from a bold bitch have been fostered onto a shy bitch and vice versa. These show quite conclusively that fear of any sort, and gun shyness in particular, is transmitted to the puppies by the time they are three or four weeks old.

Recent study has shown that in the first few weeks of their lives puppies learn much more than was previously believed. This has nothing to do with training, but simply with the conditions surrounding the puppy in its early life. By the time the puppy is eight weeks old, its instinct to keep its 'nest' clean can either be well developed or completely killed. Socialization with human beings should be developed from the time the puppy's eyes are open. At one time it was considered bad for puppies to be petted and fondled by children, but a puppy which is used to being handled from an early age will settle into its new home much more quickly. Provided it goes to the right home, the sooner the puppy leaves its brothers and sisters the better. The best age is usually between seven and eight weeks old.

Supposing that you have found a litter of puppies of your chosen breed, that you like the parents and that the pups have been well reared under reasonable conditions, what should you look for in the puppy itself? First of all remember that, although the puppies may look very much alike now, they will all grow up with very different characters, just like any family of brothers and sisters. And if you have just lost one of the same breed, don't expect any of these puppies to grow up just like your old dog.

In nearly every litter there is a dominant puppy which is quicker to learn than the others – very often learning how to escape! It is usually, but not invariably, a dog and as soon as the pups can crawl it will be first out of the nest, first to the feed bowl and almost certainly first to greet you on arrival. In later life this puppy will probably be a good worker, but it will also often be very dominant and wilful, making it difficult to train. The second, or even third, puppy in the social scale is often a better choice, but a lot depends on the parents. If the parents are hard dogs, choose the most submissive puppy, but if they are very amenable, soft dogs then you want to go for a bold puppy, even the number one puppy. Take plenty of time looking at a litter of pups and discussing them with the breeder, who knows, or should know, each puppy individually. The puppy to choose is the one which comes to you when you squat down to speak to it, which snuggles up to you when you take it in your arms, and which does not run away if you clap your hands or make an unexpected movement. The puppy you should leave behind is the independent dog which stalks off, minding its own business, which struggles to get out of your arms when you pick it up, and which runs away when you clap your hands. And the puppy you should not have on any account is the one which, on seeing a stranger, runs into its kennel or hides in a corner. Many people, especially women, feel sorry for a shy puppy and buy it, only to regret having done so for the rest of the dog's life. It is also very cruel to keep a nervous dog in a house full of rowdy children or any other noisy conditions. To force an animal to live in constant fear of everything around it is surely just as cruel as if you were to beat or starve it.

Always look for a dog with a bright, bold eye which looks straight at you honestly, and avoid any dog with a shifty, furtive look. Bright eyes are a guide to physical well-being as well as temperament, and it is equally important to start with a healthy puppy. Its skin should be soft and pliable when picked up in the hand and its coat should be glossy, although some types of coat do not look glossy even when in the best condition. The skin should be free from sores and bare patches, which can be due to fleas or lice, usually easily cured, but sometimes caused by a type of mange which may be impossible to cure. If the puppy is potbellied it is probably due to worms which are also easy to treat, but it is a sign of neglect, or ignorance, on the part of the breeder as the pup should have been wormed before this stage.

Opposite: Although children should be encouraged to make friends with their pets, they should not be allowed to go too far. Apart from the question of hygiene, it can be very dangerous to put your face close to a strange dog or a nervous puppy and many children have been badly bitten by doing so.

Below: A Spitz puppy with its young owner in Finland.

Right: A young Sealyham puppy, rather uncertain on its feet.

Below: Young Dalmatians at play.

Opposite page: This Poodle bitch suckling her puppies is obviously a contented and affectionate mother.

Right: A Beagle puppy setting out on the path of life.

Below: Golden Retriever puppies are very appealing at this age.

The most important point to remember with a young puppy is that it is still a baby. It is surprising how many people overlook this fact. They have some idea that if they don't start training their puppy right away, it can never be trained. At this age, however, the puppy does not need a replacement pack leader so much as a replacement mother. This is why women are so much better than men at rearing puppies. There is no such thing as giving a puppy too much affection, but don't forget that, like all babies, it needs a lot of sleep. Much suffering is caused to puppies which go to new homes where children are allowed to maul and play with them continuously. Many people would do well to train their children before attempting to cope with a dog!

New owners often make the mistake of starting to house train the puppy the moment they get it home. They take this infant from its brothers and sisters and its familiar surroundings, probably on a long car journey, then put it down on the kitchen floor, whereupon it does what any sensible person would expect it to do and the owner immediately smacks it for leaving a puddle on the floor. But animals do not reason as we do, they learn by association of ideas, and rather than associating the punishment with the 'crime' as the owner intended, the puppy is more likely to associate the punishment with the person who administered it and with its new home in general. This kind of treatment turns many bold, friendly puppies into timid, nervous wrecks within a few days of going to a new home. It never ceases to amaze us that mothers will wrap their own child in nappies, yet expect a canine infant to go through the night without relieving itself.

The best way to learn how to take over from the puppy's mother is to study her behaviour. She is constantly licking and caressing her puppies and pushing them about in play. We are not suggesting that you start licking your new charge, but a tense or worried puppy will often relax immediately in response to the touch of a sensitive and sympathetic hand. The bitch also 'talks' to her puppies in very soft tones, usually inaudible to human ears, so try to talk to your puppy in a quiet, reassuring tone of voice. This does not mean subjecting it to a barrage of meaningless chatter; talk to it when there is a reason for doing so and try to get some response.

If a puppy annoys its mother, say by biting too hard in play, she will growl at it and, if that has no effect, snap at it. Next time she growls at the puppy, it will associate the sound with correction and stop whatever it is doing. A sudden snap from the bitch is reserved for more serious misbehaviour. It nearly always frightens the puppy, and it will almost certainly draw back and may even run away. But very soon it will come back and probably roll on its back in front of her. Her response to this is to lick and caress the puppy, making friendly noises and reassuring it in every way she can that she still loves it – so long as it behaves itself.

The human 'mother' can, and should, learn several things from this behaviour. The bitch corrects the puppy *as and when* it is doing the wrong thing; not several seconds or even minutes after, as so many humans do. And once the puppy has been corrected, it is over and all is forgiven. Very soon the puppy associates a growl with correction, and will stop whatever it is doing. A puppy reacts instinctively to a growl, and it is very seldom that a puppy will go right up to a strange dog which growls at it. This instinct can be, and should be, used in training.

To give a practical example of how this treatment should work with your puppy, imagine it is chewing the hearth rug. You should say 'No' to it in a harsh 'growling' tone (never shout – the puppy has better hearing than you). A sensitive puppy will probably react to this growl and stop chewing, whereupon you should praise it by stroking it and encouraging it in a friendly tone. If it does not respond to the growl, follow immediately with correction which, for a puppy of this age, can be a light tap on the nose or gripping the scruff of its neck. As soon as the puppy responds, praise it well. A lively puppy will probably take some time to learn, but repeat the whole performance more severely each time until it gives up.

It is important to remember that 'No' is not the first sound a puppy should learn to understand. Dogs do not understand words, only sounds; it is just as easy to teach a dog to lie down by saying 'Stand up' as it is by saying 'Lie down'. The first sound a new puppy should learn is its name. It should learn to associate its name with pleasure and your first object should be to get it to come to you every time it hears its name. One of the most usual of all dog problems are dogs which will not come when they are called. Most of these dogs have been taught *not* to come, because the owner has created

Above: A working sheepdog puppy.

Left: Contrary to common belief, cats and dogs are not necessarily natural enemies.

the wrong associations. Some have been taught to run away by the owner's efforts to train them. For a young puppy in a new home, every effort should therefore be made to make it associate its name with pleasure. Later on the name can be used in different tones, but for the present it must always be spoken in a friendly, reassuring tone. Never shout the puppy's name and never use its name to scold it. Use a harsh 'No' or 'Ahh' which can be growled rather than spoken. Don't keep repeating the puppy's name, as that will simply accustom it to a sound which it will learn to ignore, like the radio or conversation. And don't call it when there is no chance whatsoever of it responding – for instance, when it is digging a hole in the garden or sees a dog in the distance. Call it when it happens to be coming in your direction of its own accord. When it reaches you, praise it enthusiastically and offer it some food. Next time the puppy hears its name, it should show more inclination to come towards you. The more you shout a puppy's name without getting any response, the more you are teaching it not to come when called.

The first thing most people want to teach a puppy is to be house clean. To the majority of owners it is much more important that the puppy should be clean in the house than that it should be happy, but a lot of people overlook the fact that a happy puppy is more likely to be clean than an unhappy one. There are two important points to remember here. First, that we are dealing with a baby, and second that, unlike some other babies, the puppy has a natural instinct to keep its living quarters clean. Babies cannot go for any length of time without emptying both bladder and bowels, and an instinct cannot develop if given no opportunity to do so. In other words, if the puppy cannot relieve itself outdoors, Nature will force it to relieve itself indoors. And once this becomes a habit, it is very difficult to break.

The first few days in a puppy's new home are vital for teaching good habits. Vigilance and time spent in the early days will be more than repaid later on. You should notice when the puppy feels uncomfortable, but you may get very little warning with a young puppy. Pick it up gently and quietly and take it out. Don't *put* it out, but *take* it out and stay with it until it does what you want it to do, then praise it and bring it indoors again.

Puppies nearly always want to relieve themselves when they wake up and after they have had a meal. So take yours out at these times, whether or not it shows any desire to do so. A puppy which has been brought up under clean conditions will soon go towards the door when it feels uncomfortable. All you have to do then is to open the door. But remember that the puppy cannot open the door itself, and it cannot wait until you come back from shopping or finish a long telephone conversation. To punish a puppy which makes a mistake under these circumstances is pointless and cruel.

Few people, however, have the time to keep a constant eye on a puppy. The answer to this is a playpen, very similar to a child's playpen, an essential piece of equipment for the average puppy owner. The pen should be placed as near as possible to the door, with a bed in one corner, and the floor should be covered with newspaper. When you are too busy to keep an eye on the puppy, all you have to do is pop it in its pen. There might appear to be a disadvantage in that the puppy will get into the habit of using the newspaper in its pen and will not want to go outside. But when the puppy is outside its pen, it will tend to go towards the pen if it wants to relieve itself. This should be fairly obvious and you can easily put it outside – hence the reason for the pen being near the door. When eventually you remove the playpen and the newspaper altogether, the puppy will still head for the same spot and you can then open the door so that it can go outside.

So far we have been dealing with the puppy brought up under good conditions, but all puppies are not brought up under good conditions, and if the instinct to be clean is not strong enough in itself, something more drastic is necessary in an effort to develop it. You will need to teach the puppy what to do and what not to do by correction and reward. If the puppy just squats down wherever it happens to be, without any warning, pick it up quickly, 'growl' at it with a harsh 'No' and take it outside. Don't smack it, but don't be as gentle as you would be with a puppy which is trying to be clean. Being picked up firmly and quickly is a severe enough correction for a young puppy. A reasonably sensitive puppy will now associate feeling uncomfortable with correction, and this will worry it and make it hesitate the next time. Now is your opportunity to pick it up gently, talking to it in reassuring tones. This will help it to understand that it is doing the right thing, and also that you are still a nice person even if you did have to correct it for doing wrong. With a less sensitive puppy, you may have to repeat the correction several times before it gets the message and you may have to be more severe, even to the extent of grabbing it by the scruff of its neck and giving it a good shake. But don't slap the puppy and don't correct it if you go into a room and find a puddle on the floor. Just wipe the mess up and wait for an opportunity to catch the puppy in the act.

The sooner a puppy is taken out to meet the great wide world, the easier it will be for it to accept it. Very young puppies are much less likely to be afraid of strange people, noise and so on, than older ones, and they are less likely to be carsick. But if you take a young puppy out before it has

been inoculated, at about the age of eight weeks, there is a grave risk of it picking up an infection. You can take a puppy out in the car from the age of six weeks, but take care not to put it on ground where other dogs have been. It can be handled and made a fuss of, but try to avoid people with dogs of their own. If you take care, the risk of infection is very small and certainly less than the risk of the puppy becoming shy of traffic and people if kept away from them for too long.

Car sickness is in itself quite a problem. Start by taking the puppy out as young as possible, as frequently as possible and for very short distances. But don't take it out just after a meal! Some dogs are never car-sick but if yours is, try to get it over the problem as quickly as possible. There are a great many tranquillizers available which will help. It is wise to consult your veterinary surgeon, who will advise on the correct drug and dosage for your particular puppy. But you should not regard drugs as a cure, only as an aid to help the puppy. Always give the minimum dose, and if it does not work, you can give a little more next time. Reduce the dose as soon as possible until you find that the puppy is quite happy without being given anything. You can also help your puppy to overcome car sickness by trying to persuade it to associate the car with pleasure. A puppy's first car ride usually takes it away from its own familiar surroundings to a new home, which it inevitably finds very bewildering. And all too often its next trip is to the vet, who sticks a needle in it. So make a regular car journey, such as driving the children to school, take the puppy with you and feed it when you get home. The children should prevent it thinking too much about itself on the way there, the journey back will be short and it will have its breakfast as a reward. It is also worth taking the puppy out in the car before giving it a walk. If you take it even a short way in the car and then let it have a romp which it enjoys, it should very soon associate the car with pleasure and be anxious to go in it. When you do have to go on a longer journey, it is often a good idea to stop after the first half hour or so and let the puppy have a good run.

Once your puppy is old enough to be inoculated (eight to twelve weeks), you should consult a veterinary surgeon as there are various types of inoculation. Two inoculations are normally given, which will protect your puppy against distemper, hardpad, hepatitis and two forms of leptospirosis.

Remember that it is not a good idea to take an uninoculated puppy into a waiting room with other dogs which may be infected; if possible, try to find a vet with an appointment system so that you can be seen immediately, or wait outside in your car.

Above left: A Norfolk Terrier puppy in a light, portable playpen.

Right: An energetic young Lhasa Apso is quite a handful, but fun to own.

Overleaf: The authors' dogs – and other animals.

Dog Breeds

Hunting to Hounds

N O one really knows how long ago it was that Man first domesticated the dog, but what does seem certain is that the first purpose for which Man used dogs was to help him hunt and kill other animals.

It is likely that Man used dogs to hunt before he actually domesticated them. From early times right up to the present day, falcons have been used for hunting, but they have never been domesticated, and there have been several instances of rat-catchers using tame foxes to help them in their work. It is probable that the first dogs used by Man were orphan cubs taken from the nest and hand-reared. These would have been only too willing to hunt and kill the other animals which at that time were essential for Man's survival.

Left: A Foxhound pack in kennels.

Right: The Devon and Somerset Staghounds.

Overleaf: The Suffolk Foxhounds.

Having realized their usefulness, Man no doubt bred from these dogs, and naturally he bred selectively, from the best stock – and the best stock to him were the best hunters. As we have already seen, one cannot put an instinct there or take it away, but one can strengthen or weaken it by selective breeding. It is for this reason that all hunting breeds have a stronger hunting instinct than any wild dog. The wild dog only kills what it needs to eat, but once the hunting instinct has been aroused in the domestic dog, it will kill and go on killing, purely for its own sake. There are authentic records of terriers killing incredible numbers of rats; for example, in the early 1820s a terrier called Billy killed 100 rats in little over 5 minutes. Unfortunately there are also records of whole flocks of sheep being killed and maimed by packs of domestic dogs. In this case the hunting instinct has been stimulated by the influence of the pack instinct, and it should always be remembered that it only takes two dogs to form a pack.

One of the remarkable things about the domestic dog is the many different shapes and sizes in which it is to be found. On looking at them, it is hard to believe that all the different breeds, from the tiny Chihuahua to the giant Irish Wolfhound, are descended from an animal whose survival depended on its ability to kill. But it is easy to understand if one studies their behaviour, and many breeds which have not been bred for hunting for centuries still retain a strong hunting instinct.

The majority of those dogs which have been bred specifically to hunt and kill their prey are all the many hounds and terriers. These breeds must form at least half the world's dog population. The hounds can be divided roughly into two groups, those which hunt by scent and those which hunt by sight. The former usually hunt in packs in much the same way as wild dogs, the main difference being that the huntsman is the pack leader.

Although hounds existed in Britain before then, most of today's British and Continental hounds are believed to be descended from a pack of hounds founded by Saint Hubert in the Ardennes in the sixth century. They were brought to England during the Norman Conquest, at the same time as the Talbot Hounds and Bloodhounds, both of which were descended from the original Saint Hubert Hounds. The Saint Hubert Hound and the Talbot are now extinct, but the Bloodhound has survived practically unchanged. Originally used to hunt such animals as deer and boars, it was found that Bloodhounds also had an extraordinary ability to track human beings. There are many records of their use (usually successful) in the days of Border fighting between Scotland and England. Today the Bloodhound is used, usually singly and on a tracking line, almost exclusively to track people, although they are sometimes also hunted in packs with mounted followers. They are used by prison authorities in many parts of the world, their task being to track down escaped criminals. Contrary to common belief, Bloodhounds do not attack their quarry and indeed usually greet him like a long-lost friend, slobbering all over him. Because of this, they are usually hunted on a tracking line so that their handler can keep up with them. Once on the track, the dog must ignore all other tracks, human or animal. Here the Bloodhound has no equal, and it is not uncommon for one to pick up a track several days old and stick to it, even when it has been crossed by several fresh tracks.

Apart from its terrific scenting abilities, the Bloodhound also excels in tone of voice, another characteristic handed down from the Saint Hubert Hound. When hounds are hunting loose, it is essential that they give tongue, otherwise they would be lost from their handler as soon as they went out of sight. But to the true huntsman the Bloodhound's call means far more than that. He talks of the 'music of hounds', which excites horses just as much as it does men. And there is no music to surpass the deep melodious tones of the Bloodhound in full cry. This very asset, however, is one of the main reasons why Bloodhounds are only used to a very limited extent by the police. They want a dog which will work quietly and which will, if necessary, pursue and capture the criminal. Working trials are held for Bloodhounds and there are also classes for them at the larger shows, so their unique tracking ability is likely to be preserved.

Man has retained his natural hunting instinct just as much as the dog, and long after it was necessary for him to hunt for food he continued, and still continues, to hunt for sport, often using hounds to help him. Stag hunting with packs of hounds was for centuries the most popular sport of the nobility throughout Britain, France and most other European countries. Many breeds and strains of hounds were crossed

Right: The Peak Bloodhounds.

Opposite page: The Waveney Harriers.

in an effort to produce dogs with better and better hunting ability. At first big, strong hounds were in favour, and as they often hunted in thick forest the ability to stick to a line was more important than speed. Then, as the forests were cleared to make room for agricultural land, a lighter, faster hound gradually developed. Today there is comparatively little staghunting, mainly because there are fewer deer, not because they have been reduced by hunting but simply because Man has removed much of their natural habitat. For the modern huntsman, the stag has been replaced by the fox.

Although there are records of foxes being hunted as far back as the thirteenth century, it was not until the mid-eighteenth century that foxhunting became a popular sport. Until then the fox was regarded as vermin, to be killed in any way possible. The first Foxhounds were bred from the Staghounds in existence at the time. They became smaller, lighter and faster than the Staghounds and great detail was, and still is, paid to breeding. Some packs have records going back to the early 1700s and the Master of Foxhounds Association has kept a stud book since 1880. That does not mean there is only one correct type of Foxhound. In open country where the followers can gallop across grassland on fast horses, hounds are required to set the pace. But in wooded country where there is rarely an opportunity to gallop far in the open, hounds are needed to stick to a line (often crossed by other foxes, deer and people) and to give tongue so that the huntsman knows where they are.

Hounds from different packs are consequently often quite different in appearance, but at the same time the hounds within one pack are remarkably alike. Although new blood is continually being introduced to any pack of hounds, a great effort is made to preserve its own type. Even colour is taken into account; while some packs are all black and tan with no white markings, others are predominantly white with only very light markings.

The main type of Foxhound is the English Foxhound, which is also the type generally found in Scotland and Ireland. There is also a Welsh Foxhound, which has a rough coat. The history of this breed seems to be lost in the dim past, but it appears certain that it is older than any of the other British hounds. The Welsh Foxhound's admirers even claim that it is descended from the original hounds of Gaul. It is noted for its good voice, tenacity and general toughness.

Not surprisingly, packs of Foxhounds have been established in America, Australia, New Zealand and many other countries. These were originally formed from importations of British and French stock and closely resemble the English Foxhounds. In America, one finds English *and* American Foxhounds. The American Foxhound is really a separate strain of the English Foxhound, suited to the country in which it hunts. In England the crime of all crimes for any foxhunter is to shoot a fox, but in some parts of America the foxhunter carries a gun and uses two or three 'foxdogs' to flush the fox out of cover, rather like a spaniel flushing game.

The history of hare hunting goes back to 350 BC, long before foxhunting and possibly even before staghunting. Harriers with mounted followers are used to hunt the hare. The history of some of the English packs goes back much further than that of Foxhounds but, like Foxhounds, the breed has been evolved from a mixture of various types of hounds. Even today there are several types of Harrier. To the layman they look like small Foxhounds and, in fact, undersized hounds are sometimes drafted from Foxhound to Harrier packs and some Harriers are used to hunt the fox as well as the hare.

The origin of the Beagle is not quite clear, but Xenophon, writing in 350 BC, described hare hunting with small hounds which sound very much like the Beagle of today. The Romans probably brought some of these Greek hounds with them to Britain and it was in Britain that the breed and the sport of beagling developed. But it was not until the reign of Henry VII that we find any further writing on the subject.

The present-day Beagle in many ways resembles a small Foxhound. Beagles vary in height from about 25–40 cm (10–16 ins), but most of the hunting packs have hounds ranging from 37–38 cm (14½–15 ins). This is big enough to catch a hare, but small enough to be followed on foot. Most are smooth-coated but the Welsh Beagle, like its Foxhound counterpart, has a rough wiry coat. The Beagle has a very good nose and 'packs' well, in other words the pack will stay together without straggling.

There is much less pomp and ceremony about beagling than there is in foxhunting. To many foxhunters, much of the enjoyment

lies in turning out in style on a well-groomed horse, but to a beagler the main object is to watch the hounds working. One has to be very keen – and fit – to run across bogs and moors in all sorts of weather, but many beaglers do just that.

In Canada and America the Beagle has become even more popular than in its native country, and the American Kennel Club registers more than 60,000 of the breed each year. Sometimes they hunt in packs to run down their quarry, the cottontail rabbit, but they are used more extensively in conjunction with guns, when their job is to push the rabbit out into the open. Their good voices enable the hunters to know when they pick up a trail, and whether the quarry is approaching or going away. In England small packs of Beagles are also sometimes used in the same way.

The Beagle has also become popular as a show and pet dog on both sides of the Atlantic. It is a smart-looking little dog, easy to keep clean and look after, but unfortunately not always so easy to train. Several small 'pocket' Beagles have been imported from America, but in fact these miniatures were not developed there. In the *Sportsman's Encyclopedia*, published in 1830, we find the following: 'and as to the very smallest distinguished by the name of lapdog beagle, though they are very pretty in appearance, and may occasionally kill a hare, yet ultimate satisfaction cannot be expected from their exertions'.

The Basset is a very old breed which has been popular for centuries on the Continent, particularly in France. It was originally used to hunt wild boar, deer and wolves. There are several different types,

some with quite straight legs and some with very crooked legs, some with smooth coats and some with rough. All bear a strong resemblance to the Bloodhound in shape of head, voice and scenting ability.

The first Bassets were not introduced to Britain until 1866, when the Marquis of Tourman presented a pair to Lord Galway. They quickly became popular as show dogs and among their many distinguished breeders was the late Queen Alexandra who kept both rough- and smooth-coated Basset breeds. There were many importations at that time, the smooths being of the low, crooked-legged variety (*Basset à jambes tortues*) and the roughs of the half-crooked kind (*Basset à jambes semi-tortues*). For some reason, the Basset Griffon Vendéen never became popular and most of the Bassets shown today in Britain and America are of the smooth variety.

It was not until 1884 that Bassets were first used for hunting hare in Britain and, although a few packs have been in existence since then, they have never become nearly as popular as the Beagle. This is probably because they are much more independent dogs and do not hunt so well as a pack. Nevertheless, they are terrific hunters and the music of a pack of Bassets in full cry is worth going a long way to hear. In America and in Europe the Basset is used more as a gun dog, to find and push game out of thick cover.

Bassets have great character and their appearance is often deceptive. They are not soulful, quiet or lazy dogs, indeed they are probably the toughest and most persistent of all the scenting hounds. Once a Basset gets its nose onto a line, it is oblivious to

everything else and some have even been known to hunt until they dropped dead from exhaustion. They are also much bigger and more powerful dogs than people imagine. Though only 30–38 cm (12–15 ins) at the shoulder they weigh up to 22.5 kg (50 lbs), about twice the weight of a Beagle of the same height. Because of its very short legs the Basset is not very fast for its size, but this can also be deceptive, as many owners of wayward Bassets can testify! Its lack of speed is compensated for by sheer courage and determination, which make it crash its way through the thickest gorse or thorn, water or bog.

Otterhunting is a very old sport in Britain, the first known Master of Hounds being King Henry II. Queen Elizabeth I also had a pack of Otterhounds and was probably the first lady Master of Hounds. Many other members of the Royal Family hunted the otter, the last being Charles II. In appearance the Otterhound resembles a rough-coated Bloodhound and in some ways it also resembles the Welsh Foxhound. Its colour varies from black to light grey and from red to pale fawn. There are no white markings but the colours are often mixed, for example, black and tan, grey and fawn, and so on.

Otters of up to 16 kg (35 lbs) have been recorded, and even when much smaller than this the animal is a very formidable enemy. As well as its razor-sharp slashing teeth, it has powerful claws which can inflict very severe injuries. Otters are very agile on land, and even more agile in the water, so an Otterhound must be tough, really tough. It may have to swim for hours on end and it may have to stand shivering on the

riverbank for equally long periods. And when the hound does come to grips with the otter, it will not be able to kill it with one snap like it would a fox or a hare. Like the badger, the otter has a tough skin and will fight to the bitter end, often inflicting severe injuries on its adversary. Otters have sadly become very scarce in Britain, as a result of which very few packs of Otterhounds remain. Those which do seldom consist entirely of Otterhounds, being mixed with drafted Foxhounds, Staghounds and crosses between all three.

Now we come to the hounds which hunt by sight – the Gazehounds, as they are sometimes called. These dogs were bred to hunt a wide variety of quarry in open country where it could easily be seen. Instead of following the trail by scent, they could see their quarry and simply streaked after it. Speed and determination consequently became the number one priority. Stamina was also necessary, but obviously the very fast dog which could catch a hare in 500 m (550 yds) needed a lot less stamina than a slower dog which had to pursue it for 1,000 m (1,100 yds).

Above: The Taw Vale Beagles.

Right: Many more Beagles are now kept as pets than for their original role as hunters.

The history of the Greyhound goes back much further than that of the hounds which hunt by scent, and it is much more authentic. This is not so much because these hounds have been used by Man for a longer period, but simply because they originated in the East where history itself goes back much further. Several types of Greyhound were in existence thousands of years ago, the only real differences being in the coat and the shape of the ears. Otherwise the physical structures were almost identical, which is not so surprising when one considers that they were all bred for the same purpose – speed. Egyptian monuments show hunting scenes over 4,000 years ago, in the days of the Pharaohs, with hounds exactly as we find them today. The very first treatise on any breed of dog was written by Arrian at the beginning of the Christian era. Not only does he describe the dogs then as being very similar to the Greyhounds we know today, he also describes coursing which sounds almost identical to that practised right up to the present time. In particular, he stressed the point that the killing of the hare was unimportant; the object was to test the speed and skill of one dog against another.

In Britain the Greyhound has been written about and mentioned in the Laws of the Land since the days of Canute. In 1610 there was a law stating that 'No meane person may keep any Greyhounds', and before Magna Carta the punishment for killing a Greyhound was the same as for murdering a man. Until quite recent times the keeping of a Greyhound was a very important status symbol. A government proclamation made at Sydney, Australia, in 1804 ordered the destruction of all dogs 'except greyhounds and sheepdogs'.

Elizabeth I was very keen on coursing and in 1776 the first public coursing match was held at Swaffham in Norfolk. In 1836 the first Waterloo Cup Meeting was held at Altcar near Liverpool, and this is still regarded in the same esteem as the Derby in horse racing. In 1858 the National Greyhound Coursing Club was founded in Britain and drew up strict rules for the sport. The Greyhound Stud Book was started in 1882 and all Greyhounds have to be registered in it if they are to compete at recognized coursing matches in Britain. During the nineteenth century attempts were made to popularize coursing in enclosed grounds. The hare was released at one end of a long enclosure, which had an

Above: A Bassett Griffon Vendéen.

Left: The Dumfriesshire Otterhounds, one of the few packs consisting entirely of the old type of rough-coated hound.

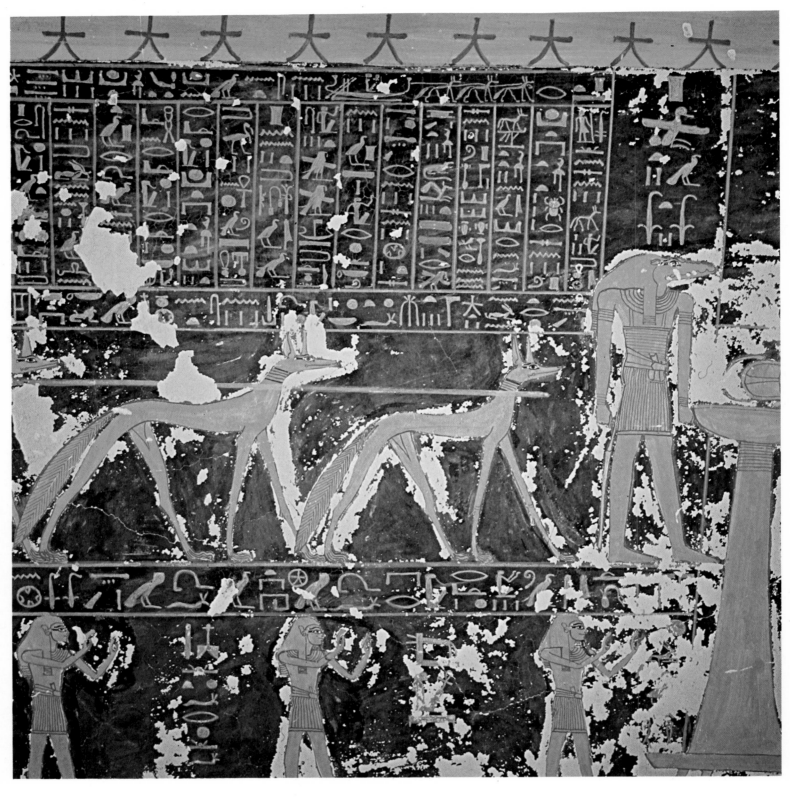

Above: A wall painting from the tomb of Ramasses VI in the Valley of Kings in Egypt, showing hunting dogs built on very similar lines to the present-day Greyhound.

Opposite page: A racing Greyhound in action on the track at Wembley Stadium.

escape hole at the other end. This was simply a test of speed, as the dogs either caught the hare before it reached the hole or it escaped. If they turned the hare before it reached the hole, it would be completely lost with no chance of escape. This method never became popular in England, although it is still used in Ireland, and is now against the rules of the National Coursing Club. It is also illegal in Britain to offer any captive wild animal to dogs for them to chase and/ or kill.

Coursing in Britain, Spain, Australia and other Commonwealth countries is conducted on very similar lines, with two dogs competing against each other in heats. Each brace is put into 'slips', which are two collars attached to each other by a long lead with a special mechanical device incorporated. When a handle is pulled, both

dogs are released simultaneously and the collars fall to the ground. The 'slipper', a highly skilled expert, takes the two competing dogs and walks with them slightly ahead of the 'field' (spectators), which stretches out in a straight line on either side of him. When a hare gets up, the slipper hangs on to the dogs (by now going mad with excitement) until the hare has had sufficient 'lay', or start. The hare needs about 75 m (82 yds) start to give it time to get into its stride before the dogs are released. It is here that the slipper's expertise comes in; two young dogs would never catch up with a strong hare if it had that much start, but on the other hand two experienced dogs would kill a weaker hare without any chance to test their real ability. The judge follows behind the dogs mounted on horseback.

The first recorded Greyhound race using an artificial hare was held in Britain in 1867, in a field at Hendon, north of London. Surprisingly enough, it did not catch on, although the inaugural meeting appears to have been popular and well-attended. In 1890 the Americans made another attempt to popularize the idea, on the horse-race track at Miami. Again it failed to receive support and it was not until 1909 that the first successful track opened at Tucson, Arizona. In 1926 an American, Charles Mann, successfully introduced the new sport to Britain and the first track was opened at Belle Vue, Manchester. In 1928 the British National Greyhound Racing Club was formed and in America there is the National Coursing Association. Greyhound racing has since become one of the most popular sports in Britain, America,

Australia and many other countries. It is often described as the 'working man's racing', but it is also patronized by the rich and the aristocracy, though perhaps not to such a great extent as coursing.

In evolving the Greyhound, Man has bred for performance and performance only. Although individual breeders had preferences for different colours and types, the dog that was used for breeding was primarily the one with the greatest speed and agility. It was left to Nature to decide what the dog should look like, and fortunately the result is aesthetically pleasing as well as fast. No breed of dog is more beautifully balanced or more symmetrical than a Greyhound. Streamlined from the tip of its nose to the tip of its tail, it is as superb a racing machine as the racehorse which has been bred on the same lines – for performance rather than appearance. A Greyhound travelling somewhere in the region of 50 km/h (31 mph) can pick up a hare without stopping or losing balance. With the aid of its long sinuous neck and strong jaws, it will break the back of its quarry and kill it more quickly than any man-made device. The old adage about a good horse never being a bad colour is also true of the Greyhound, which can be found in practically every canine colour from pure white to pure black. We find reds, fawns and blues, either whole-coloured or with white markings and brindles.

This beautiful animal has found many admirers who want to show it, and classes at the leading dog shows are quite well filled. But the standard is what Man thinks the perfect specimen should look like, and we have never heard of a winner in the showring which was also successful in the coursing field. As a pet and companion, the Greyhound can be very good or very bad. In the home it is very affectionate, intelligent and quite easy to train. Its short coat carries little mud, and in spite of its size it can curl up in a remarkably small space. But out of the house it can become an entirely different animal. Its highly developed – often over-developed – hunting instinct completely overrules any training the dog has had, and many cats and small dogs have been killed by Greyhounds.

It is easy to obtain adult Greyhounds from race tracks which are either too old or too slow for racing. There are a number of societies constantly trying to find homes for these dogs. Some of them have been reared on farms where, as puppies, they

were familiarized with and taught not to chase poultry, cats and so on. Provided they are treated sensibly and given sufficient exercise, these dogs will usually settle down and make delightful pets. But some have never had any individual attention and the only instinct that really mattered to them was the hunting instinct. Suddenly taken out of its familiar environment, such a dog will often chase and kill anything that moves.

Another coursing breed which looks very much like a small Greyhound is the Whippet. A hundred years or so ago the breed was hardly known outside the north of England and the Midlands. There the miners used them as rabbiting dogs and later started to race them to 'the rag', usually over a course of 200 yds (183 m) which the dogs frequently covered in 12 seconds. Today they are still coursed and raced, but they are also very popular as pet dogs and in the show ring.

A fit Whippet is a beautifully balanced little dog, combining elegance and grace with muscular power and strength, and moving over the ground like a Thoroughbred. Its short, easily cared-for coat, gentle nature and adaptable temperament make it an ideal companion in either town or country, but remember this is a dog which really needs to stretch its legs and a daily run is a must if you want a fit, mentally alert pet.

There seems to be no authentic history as to when the Deerhound first reached Scotland or where it came from, and it is often very difficult to differentiate between legend and history. The English historian Holinshed tells how certain Pictish nobles went hunting with Crainlint, King of the Scots, and found that his hounds were much better than their own. The King duly presented some of his hounds to them, but he was careful to keep his best hound, the one the Picts really wanted. So they stole it and a bloody battle ensued, resulting in the death of 'sixty Scott gentlemen' and over a hundred Picts. Another famous story about the breed tells of the hounds Help and Hold, which belonged to Sir William St Clare in the days of King Robert the Bruce. Apparently Sir William was given to boasting about the abilities of these hounds, while the King had no hounds worth boasting about. So the King issued a challenge that they should pull down a 'white faunch deer' on Pentland Moor, not far from Edinburgh. 'Pentland Moor is yours if your hounds hold her and your head is off

if they lose her' was the ultimatum. There must have been considerable excitement all round and some misgivings in the mind of Sir William when the stag jumped into the march burn, the stream forming the boundary of the moor. But Help and Hold plunged into the water and pulled the stag down before it reached the other side. Thus Sir William kept his head and gained the whole of Pentland Moor as well.

The old writers refer to the Deerhound as the Scottish Greyhound or Highland Greyhound and it is more than likely that they were originally the same breed but that a strain of big, strong, hairy dogs was developed to hunt the deer and a smooth, smaller strain to hunt the hare. Not surprisingly, the one developed in Scotland where deer were plentiful and the other in England where hares were plentiful.

At one time great deer drives took place, with Highland chieftains killing enormous numbers of deer. These hunts decreased with the reduction in the number of deer and the advent of sheepfarming, and ended altogether with the introduction of the rifle. When stalking first started, Deerhounds were used regularly to pursue wounded deer, but this practice has largely died out and very few, if any, are kept for that purpose today. Although they have been used in many parts of the world to

Above left: An Ibizan Hound on its native island.

Above: A stalker in Sutherland with his Deerhound.

Opposite page, left: Salukis playing on a sandy beach. They seem unable to resist the urge to gallop at full speed on sand.

Opposite page, right: A pair of long-limbed Whippets.

hunt boar, wolves and many other animals, the breed has never become very strong numerically. It was one of Queen Victoria's favourite breeds and this helped to revive it at a time when its numbers had become very low. It gained popularity not so much as a hunting dog, but as a companion and a status symbol. Because of its size, the breed does not fit very well into modern city life and is unlikely ever to become very popular today, but for anyone who wants a handsome dog and has the room to keep it the Deerhound makes a staunch, devoted companion.

Hare coursing matches are held for Deerhounds in Scotland and England. It is interesting to note that nearly all competitors are also breeders and that nearly all the winning hounds are also winners in the show ring, in marked contrast to the show Greyhound.

The history of the Saluki goes back further and with more authenticity than that of any other breed of dog. Carvings and paintings have been found in Egyptian tombs dating back to 5–6000 BC, depicting animals exactly like the present-day Saluki. Quite a number of mummified bodies have been found in the tombs of kings, showing not only its ancient lineage but also the high esteem in which it was held.

To the Arab all dogs are unclean, but to him the Saluki is not a dog. Like his horse it is his most treasured possession, sharing his tent, his food and in fact his whole life. Even today an Arab sheik visiting a Western country and meeting a Saluki will often bow to the hound before shaking hands with the owner. Neither the dogs nor the bitches are ever allowed to mate with any other breed, and there have been instances of bitches refusing to allow any dogs near them except other Salukis. Like Arab horses, the ancestry of some of them can be traced back over thousands of years.

The Saluki has been used to course the swift gazelle since before the days of the Pharaohs, and still is used for that purpose. The sheik and his retinue rode on Arab stallions and the servants walked with the hounds. Falcons were often used to locate the gazelle, although they could not kill it. When the falcon could be seen hovering above its quarry, the Salukis would be released. Even today's Salukis, generations removed from desert stock, will spot a bird (or a plane) in the sky long before it is visible to human eyes.

Left: All the agility, grace and elegance of the breed is shown in this picture of a free-trotting Afghan.

Right: A well-groomed Afghan, obviously aware of how smart it looks. It is doubtful if the carefully cultivated tresses would last long in its native Afghanistan.

Salukis were never sold, only given as presents to special friends, which is perhaps why they took so long to reach the West. In 1895 a brace of puppies was given to Lady Florence Amhurst, but it was not until 1920, when Major-General Lance and Mr Vereker-Cowley imported several from Egypt and Mesopotamia, that the breed began to establish itself in England. It was officially recognized by the British Kennel Club in 1923.

Built on the same lines as the Greyhound and for the same purpose, the Saluki is adorned with beautiful silky feathering on its legs, ears and tail. This breaks up the hard, clean utility lines of the Greyhound and to most people presents a much more beautiful animal. If the Greyhound is the utility model, the Saluki must be the de luxe.

To own a Saluki is different from owning any other dog. Just to see it walk across the room so lightly that it hardly seems to touch the ground is quite fascinating. It resents strangers, but in an aloof and gentlemanly way. It is very intelligent, but often uses this intelligence to do what it wants, rather than what its owner wants.

An excellent guard, the haughty Saluki is much tougher than its looks imply, and it can withstand wet weather and extremes of hot and cold much better than the Greyhound.

The big weakness of the Saluki as a pet is its strong hunting instinct, developed over thousands of years. It is usually very little trouble with cats, chickens and other domestic animals, but if it sees a small object in the distance which might be a hare or rabbit, it's off! The farther away it is, the more fascinating it seems to be. To see one of these beautiful animals galloping at full speed across a wide open space is a very thrilling experience, but not always convenient at the time, even though you can be sure that if you stay in the same place, it will always return.

Some people regard the Sloughi (pronounced 'Sloogi') as a smooth variety of Saluki, and it is probable that some of the desert tribes (particularly in North Africa) favoured this type and developed it separately. Although it has only recently been recognized in England and is still unrecognized in America, the breed was recognized in Holland in 1898 and is popular as a show dog in the Low Countries and Scandinavia. The English imports have come from Holland and Sweden.

The Afghan Hound also bears a strong resemblance to the Saluki, which could indicate that at one time Salukis were taken from Egypt to Afghanistan, or it could simply mean that two breeds bred for similar purposes have developed similar characteristics. Dogs very like the Afghans of today are to be found on rock carvings in the caverns of Balkh in north-east Afghanistan, dating back to 2000 BC. Folklore claims that this is the breed which Noah took with him in the Ark and, whether or not this is so, it is obviously a very old and pure breed. Found all along the borders of northern India, the Afghan is a hunting dog suited to the very difficult terrain of this area. It has been used to hunt leopards, wolves, boars, antelopes, mountain goats, and so on, and it is doubtful if any other breed of dog could leap from boulder to boulder and scramble up sheer rock faces like an Afghan. It can jump like a cat and, although not quite as fast as a Greyhound, has a remarkable turn of speed on the flat. The long shaggy coat (never as long in working dogs as in show ones) protects the Afghan from intense cold, thorny bushes, rocks and sometimes from its quarry.

The Afghan is one of the few hounds still kept primarily to hunt, and it is also used as a guard dog. In their native country, Afghans are left out at night to guard the flocks, and they have also been used as guard dogs at military border posts.

It seems strange that a dog with such a background should end up adorning a plush flat in London or New York, or to be used as an accoutrement to the dress of some elegant fashion model. Most Afghans seem to accept this mode of life with quiet disdain, but there are some which show their resentment in no uncertain manner.

A pair of 'Afghan Barukzy Hounds' were exhibited in London in 1895, but it was not until Captain John Barff imported Zerdin from Afghanistan in 1907 that the breed started to make headway in England. In 1926 it received official recognition from the British Kennel Club and has gained in popularity ever since both as a show dog and a companion.

There is something quite fascinating about the Afghan, and it is not really surprising that many people buy one who do not really have the facilities to keep it properly. As one would expect from its background, the Afghan is really a very tough dog. A great character and very intelligent, it can be trained to a very high standard, but it is also very dominant – a leader rather than a follower – and only certain people possess the necessary willpower and determination to train it, let alone the time and energy needed to keep its exotic coat well-groomed or to give it sufficient exercise.

Two very similar hounds which have recently become known in the show ring are the Pharaoh Hound and the Ibizan Hound. Both belong to the ancient Greyhound breed, and drawings of dogs very like the Pharaoh Hounds are to be found in Egyptian temples dating back to 4000 BC.

The Ibizan Hound comes from the island of Ibiza in the Balearics, and is also to be found on the other Balearic islands. It is a useful, medium-sized hound, very active and intelligent, and hunts by scent as much as by sight. In their native islands Ibizan Hounds are used to hunt partridge, hare and rabbit as well as larger game. They retrieve and point and are sometimes hunted in packs as well as singly. Although usually thought of as smooth-coated, these hounds can be wire- or long-coated, the long coat being really a rough coat.

Both these breeds have rather long, lean heads with erect ears. The Ibizan can be red and white, tawny or whole-coloured. The Pharaoh is chestnut and white or tan and white, preferably with a white tip to the tail. Both are friendly, attractive dogs and make good companions for anyone wanting a day's rabbiting in the country.

Another breed which may seem oddly classified as a hound is the Dachshund, but not if we remember that it belongs to the Teckel group which is popular throughout

Overleaf: Hound trailing is a sport confined to the Lake District in the north-west of England. It is nevertheless extremely popular and indeed could be described as an obsession with many of its followers. The hounds used are of pure Foxhound descent and have been bred exclusively for tracking for many generations. The trail is laid by dragging along it a piece of sacking soaked in a mixture of aniseed and paraffin. This provides a powerful enough smell for the dogs to follow the trail for up to 10 miles (16 km) racing flat out.

Germany and Austria as a hunting dog. There are several different types of Teckel, some quite small and others as large as a Basset, to which breed they were probably related in the past.

There are six varieties of Dachshund – long-haired, smooth-haired and wire-haired in standard sizes, and the same varieties in miniature. The ideal weight of the Miniature Dachshund is under 4.5 kg (10 lbs). Queen Victoria's husband, Prince Albert, brought several of the breed from Germany when he came to England. They very quickly caught on in England and soon afterwards in America.

In German, Dachshund means 'badger dog' and all Dachshunds are essentially sporting dogs, with excellent scenting powers and plenty of courage. Long and low, with a bold carriage, intelligent expression and lively character, they are now very popular as pets and in the show ring, but are not used to any great extent as workers outside their native country, which is rather a pity. Most Dachshunds are very determined little characters and, whilst by no means unintelligent, are not always too willing to co-operate. They come in a great variety of colours. The smooth-coated ones tend to feel the cold and will appreciate a warm jacket on a cold winter's day.

Last but definitely not least among the hounds is the Irish Wolfhound, the tallest dog in the world. At one time the breed nearly became extinct, but it is now numerically quite strong. Legend has it that the Irish hero Fionn mae Cumwell had an aunt who was turned into a hound by her enemy. Fionn managed to get her restored to human form but was not successful with her twin children, born when she was a hound. These two, Bran and Sceolaun, became his devoted companions – and the first Irish Wolfhounds. At one time they were used to hunt and kill wolves, which were so prevalent in Ireland in the 1650s that Oliver Cromwell forbade the export of Wolfhounds. Today there are no more wolves to hunt and, standing about 90 cm (35 ins) high and weighing over 45 kg (100 lbs), Wolfhounds are not the fastest of hounds after hare. For someone who can spare the room to house them, the money to feed them and the time and space to exercise them, they make devoted, gentle companions. And, although far from aggressive, they make excellent guards, their majestic size and dark eyes peering out from shaggy brows being enough to put off any intruder.

Left: A Borzoi on the track of game.

Opposite page, centre: Dachshunds rarely lose their sporting instincts, even when they have been kept as pets for several generations. They relish any opportunity to go to ground – or partly to ground.

Opposite page, bottom: This laughing Dachshund has obviously enjoyed its digging.

Below: An Irish Wolfhound on the shores of its native country.

Terriers

AFTER the hounds, the terriers are probably the best known of the hunting dogs. They come in a tremendous variety of shapes, colours, sizes and coat textures and have been native to the British Isles for centuries.

In the fifteenth century, Dame Juliana Berners, Prioress of Sopwell Nunnery, wrote, rather surprisingly, a book on field sports, in which she classified 'Teroures' as a breed used in field sports. In 1576 John Caius, physician to Queen Elizabeth, wrote a treatise on English dogs where he also mentions 'Terrarius or Terrars' as 'dogges serving y pastime of hunting beasts'. He described how their work caused them to creep underground in pursuit of foxes and badgers. So the twentieth-century terriers that bolt foxes and rabbits and kill rats are doing the same work as their ancestors of over 400 years ago.

Most people's idea of a 'Terour' is the well-known Fox Terrier. Very popular as a show dog and companion in the 1920s and 30s, it is still seen in well-filled classes at shows but not so often as a family pet. For some unknown reason, the Wire Fox Terrier has always been more popular than the Smooth. The Smooth is very easy to keep clean and tidy, although when it is casting it leaves large quantities of short white hairs all over the carpet, but the Wire needs professional trimming to be presented in the show ring and expensive visits to the beauty salon to remain a smart pet dog.

Although Dame Juliana's treatise mentioned both Smooth and Rough Terriers, it is difficult to trace their ancestry. For centuries packs of hounds have kept hunt terriers but only a few have kept records of their breeding. It is from the terriers of these packs that the modern Fox Terrier is descended. From the mid-1850s to the 1870s many of these working terriers appeared at early dog shows.

Someone once said of the old Bull Terrier that 'To own a fighting dog you must be a fighting man' and to own a terrier and appreciate it you must be 'a terrier man'. And the Reverend Dr Rosslyn Bruce described them thus: 'Of all God's creatures, animals are easily the highest; of all animals terriers are undoubtedly the most useful; of all terriers Fox Terriers are probably the most desirable; a Smooth Fox Terrier is the most heavenly thing on earth.' The modern show Fox Terrier has changed a great deal from those early days and not many show champions would be allowed to have a go at bolting foxes or killing rats even if they wanted to. Many terriers, however, still retain their sporting instincts and make merry, happy companions.

Opposite page: Terrier racing, using traps similar to those used on Greyhound tracks.

Left: A Wire Fox Terrier trimmed and ready for the show ring.

Below: Maybe not as smart as his cousin above, this Fox Terrier shows more in common with his hunting ancestors.

A terrier, like a hound, needs a good voice so that it can keep in touch with the huntsmen when it is working. Once a terrier has marked its quarry underground, it should keep on barking to let the men on the surface know its whereabouts. They can then dig down and come to grips with the fox or badger. A silent dog can easily be lost or injured underground and never heard of again. The tendency of many of the smaller terriers to enjoy the sound of their own voices is, however, not always appreciated by owners today, who no longer want to work them.

Although so well known, the Fox Terrier cannot claim pride of place in the terrier group. This must surely go to the 'king of terriers', the large Airedale from Yorkshire. It is generally accepted that the breed originated in the locality of the River Aire near Bradford in Yorkshire, and that it was a mixture of Otterhound and various

local terriers. Known originally as the 'Waterside Terrier', it excelled at water work such as catching water voles. But it was soon discovered that this large terrier, weighing about 22½ kg (50 lbs) was the ideal all-round sportsman. The only thing it could not do was go to ground, but it would have a go at anything else. It could catch rabbits, kill rats, swim like an otter, mark game, retrieve, work on the farm, act as nursemaid to the children, and was a very reliable family guard. Small wonder then that it became so popular in many countries. In 1884 the breed was classified by the British Kennel Club and exported all over the world. Apart from becoming a popular show dog in America, an Airedale won the first police dog trials held in Madison Square Gardens. In Africa Airedales hunted water buck and bush buck, in France they hunted wild boar, and they became well known as police dogs in Britain and Germany. They even acted as war dogs during World War I. It seems sad that this game, intelligent, good-looking dog should now be low down in the popularity stakes, and that they are now only used as police dogs in Germany. But fashions keep changing in the dog world as everywhere else, and it is to be hoped that the Airedale will once again resume its rightful position as the king of terriers.

Two other large terriers which are not used for going to ground are the Kerry Blue and the Soft-Coated Wheaten, both Irishmen. The latter is said to be the oldest and the Kerry is believed to be descended from it, but both breeds can be traced back 200 years or more. Medium-sized dogs of around 15 kg (35 lbs), they have a number of similarities. The coat in both breeds should be soft, wavy and silky, any shade of blue in the Kerry and a light clear wheaten in the Soft-Coated Wheaten. For the show ring the Kerry is trimmed and clipped to a specific pattern. Its soft coat is not stripped like a number of other terrier breeds but clipped, more like a Poodle coat. If you don't want your pet Kerry to resemble a blue sheep, its coat will need a considerable amount of time spent on it – or money, if you have it professionally trimmed. The abundant coat of the Soft-Coated Wheaten is usually left untrimmed, which may save the cost of visits to the beauty salon but still costs a lot of time and trouble to keep it in order. If left ungroomed it quickly becomes matted, not only looking unsightly but possibly causing sores to develop under the mats.

The Kerry Blue, originally known as the Irish Blue, was first shown in Killarney in Ireland in 1915 and at Crufts in 1922, but the Wheaten was not recognized in Britain until 1939. In Ireland the Kerry was, and in some cases still is, used to herd cattle, catch rats, play with the children, guard the farm, as well as being expected to do any other job that came along. It has a reputation for 'playfulness', which not all owners would appreciate. Both dogs show plenty of terrier character and need firm handling, but in the right hands they make excellent guards and loyal companions. Neither, however, is a breed for anyone who does not want to spend time and trouble on grooming and training.

Another Irishman is the smaller Irish Terrier. Weighing about 10–13 kg (24–29 lbs) with a harsh red or red wheaten coat, it fully justifies its title of 'Daredevil' and will not be put upon by lesser dogs. The Irish Terrier is a smart-looking dog, and should be trimmed for show in a similar pattern to the Fox Terrier. Built on more racy lines than most terriers, it is usually an excellent ratter and has been known to work quite well in the shooting field. It is a merry, affectionate dog but, like most other terriers, will soon get into mischief if left with nothing to do. Its rather reckless pluck can be more of a liability than an asset at times.

Scotland also has its quota of terriers which have been known there for many centuries. It was not until the late nineteenth century, however, that the various types became separated and known by names such as the Aberdeen (now the Scottish Terrier), Dandie Dinmont, West Highland White, Skye and Cairn.

Rather like the wild Irish Terrier, the Scottie seems to have acquired some of the characteristics of its native countrymen. A Scotsman once wrote of it: 'Jock should be a thinker, a philosopher and a seer; his soul is oppressed by the crass stupidity of all things created, and he shows it on his countenance. A Scottish terrier should look like a Kirk Elder the morning after a glorious fuddle – remorse, for hard-earned money squandered and time wasted.' For all that, this dour wee terrier has a number of devoted followers. Although commonly thought of as black, the Scottish Terrier can also be wheaten and brindle. It is an independent little chap, well able to look after itself, and at times appears rather sedate. Readily adaptable to town life, its coat does not show the dirt and it is a hardy little dog which needs little fussing over.

Opposite page: Smooth Fox Terriers, similar to their wire-haired cousins but their smooth coats are less trouble to groom.

Left: A neatly trimmed Irish Terrier. Although there are differences to the expert eye, the trim is very similar to that of the Wire Fox Terrier.

Like most terriers, it is a good guard dog with a deep bark for its size.

The West Highland White has a harsh weather-resistant coat, trimmed for show but more on the lines of the Cairn and not as barbered as the Scottish Terrier. It should not carry a great deal of coat and the pet Westie will need stripping down to its undercoat about twice a year. In between times, a good daily brushing should keep it looking and feeling in order. Appealing, cheeky, self-confident small dogs, West Highland Whites are usually very adaptable and do not seem to mind living in town houses and flats. It is believed they were originally throw-outs from Cairn litters, as white Cairns were disliked.

The late Baroness Burton once said, 'Cairns have no disadvantages.' Certainly they have as many advantages today as when she wrote that over 50 years ago. A hardy, intelligent breed, they are only small, some weighing as little as 4 kg (9 lbs). Many still work with hounds and quite a number of show Cairns hold a Master of Foxhounds working certificate. Even so, they seem quite happy living in towns. Their harsh coat, with its thick undercoat, keeps out the weather and needs very little attention from the professional trimmer. Colours vary from light wheaten to nearly black. For someone wanting a small but sporting dog, the Cairn takes a lot of beating.

Although the birthplace of the Skye Terrier was the Island of Skye, it was not actually given the name until 1861. They are rather out of favour today, except as show dogs, which may be because of their long flowing coats which require a great deal of attention. But it should be remembered that the pet Skye does not carry the excessive coat of the show dogs, and it takes a great deal of time, patience and experience to develop the glistening blue or fawn curtain, carefully parted in the centre, which hangs straight down on either side of the body. It is fairly obvious that a dog with such a coat would not keep it looking that way for long after a day's rabbiting. The Skye is a stolid little dog, very loyal to its own family but not overkeen on strangers. It makes a good housedog if you can spare the time to look after its coat, which can bring in a lot of mud on wet days as it is very near to the ground.

Another terrier from Scotland with a unique character and appearance is the Dandie Dinmont. Tough little terriers were used for most kinds of sport in the Border Country between Scotland and England long before Sir Walter Scott created a fictional character called Dandie Dinmont who kept a pack of useful pepper- or mustard-coloured terriers. A bright Border farmer called James Davidson had a strain of terriers which closely resembled Scott's description and so he started calling them Dandie Dinmonts. They sold very well and soon they were being exhibited at dog shows. The Dandie is a quaint little fellow with a weasel-shaped body, short sturdy legs, a large head with dark expressive eyes and a soft silky topknot, adding up to an unusual but attractive little terrier which tends to look larger than it is. Even its deep, resonant voice gives the impression of a larger breed. The Dandie is still a game, fearless little dog and, as Sir Walter Scott wrote, 'They fear nothing that ever cam wi' a hairy skin on't.' Perhaps, though, it is really more at home in the country than the city.

A little farther south from Scotland is the home of the Border and Bedlington Terriers. The Bedlington probably shares the same ancestry as the Dandie but it is believed to have been crossed with Whippets to give it more speed to catch rabbits in the open. It arrived in the show ring in 1869 and, although quite popular in the early twentieth century, it is not seen so much nowadays. The Bedlington is quite a tall terrier, about 38–41 cm (15–16 ins), with long legs, a long neck and a long domed head crowned with a silky topknot, reminiscent of the Dandie. Its coat is what is called 'twisty', which is really a mixture of hard and soft hair. It is not the easiest of coats to keep in good trim, and a pet Bedlington will need professional attention at regular intervals. Its looks are inclined to make some people think it is a soft dog but this is mistaken. The real Bedlington is a very sporting terrier, intelligent and easier to train than some of the other, more independent breeds.

The Border Terrier has survived the transition from working terrier to show dog with little change. It is an ideal little dog for someone wanting a natural-looking terrier which needs the minimum of attention to keep it smart. Its short, hard coat is coloured red, wheaten, grizzle, tan, or blue and tan. Its head is a bit unlike the other terriers, being more otter-shaped. The Border's racy build enables it to run with hounds, and yet it is small enough to go to ground. It is a keen, plucky little dog

which will tackle anything that moves. Two Border Terriers which were exported to Canada would tackle any game including porcupine, and their owner reported that they had once done 110 km (70 miles) in the hills running with the horses. They are still used by some Foxhound packs, and they also make excellent small sporting companions.

Although classified as a toy dog, the Yorkshire Terrier is still a terrier, if a diminutive one. This tiny Yorkshireman has had a spectacular rise to popularity during the past 50 years, and there are probably few countries in the world where it is not shown and kept as a pet. Today it is a tiny dog of under 3 kg (7 lb) in weight – – many show-winners weigh less than half that – but years ago its larger predecessor could be found all over the Yorkshire moors and dales, keeping down the rats on the farms. Many of this old-fashioned sort are still seen in their native county.

To develop the glamorous, long silky coat of the show-winner, the modern Yorkshire Terrier must live a somewhat restricted life. But the pet Yorkie seldom carries as much coat and is often slightly larger than the show type, probably a bit tougher too. Its shorter coat does not need too much attention to keep it in good trim and it is a handy-sized dog to keep in a town flat. Yorkshire Terriers are loyal, active little dogs, not over-keen on unsolicited advances from strangers and not averse to telling them so with a sharp nip from their minute teeth. Like a number of terriers, they rather like the sound of their own voices, but being bright, intelligent little dogs they are usually very easily trained.

Two other very natural-looking little dogs are the Norwich and the Norfolk Terriers. Until 1965 both types, drop- and prick-eared, were called Norwich Terriers and in Britain were put in the same classes at shows; they are still classified as Norwich Terriers in America. In their native counties they worked with Foxhounds and they also became very popular in America as workers. But in 1965 it was decided to call the drop-eared type the Norfolk Terrier, while the prick-eared type remained the Norwich. So a new breed was given official recognition, when in fact it was already well established in the show ring. They are among the smaller terriers, standing about 25 cm (10 ins) high, and both breeds have hard, straight, wiry coats which need the minimum of trimming. Their

Opposite page: A West Highland White Terrier, looking very well groomed.

Top: An Airedale Terrier in Switzerland accompanies his master on a cross-country skiing expedition.

Above: The popular Scottish Terrier. This one is neatly trimmed but not over-barbered.

colour can be any shade of red, grizzle, or black and tan. They are both compact, jaunty little dogs, not usually aggressive, and they make affectionate companions which seem quite happy to live in town or country.

To most people the Lakeland Terrier looks like a coloured Fox Terrier, and at early shows in the Lake District these local dark-coloured terriers were classified as 'Coloured Working Terriers' and the rest as 'White Fox Terriers'. Lakelands were used, and still are used, to run with the packs of hounds used to hunt foxes in the rocky Fell country. These packs have foot followers, not a mounted field, as the country is too rough for horses. The Lakeland will go underground and bolt a fox, or if the fox goes into hiding in a rocky 'borran' the terrier is expected to go in after it and

either put it out for the hounds or kill it there on its own. So this is a really tough dog which prefers to have a job of work to do, preferably a hard job with plenty of action. Its hard wiry coat is trimmed for shows very much the same as the Wire Fox Terrier. There are various colours for the Lakeland, including black and tan, wheaten and grizzle. Should you decide to keep one in the town, it will not show the dirt too much and is a handy size, but remember that there is still plenty of terrier character there and it will need to be kept occupied.

A breed often confused with the Lakeland is the Welsh Terrier, one of the oldest varieties of terrier in Britain. Although it has never gained the popularity of the more flashy-coloured Wire Fox Terrier, it is still quite well known and has gained success in the American show ring.

Below: This cheerful little Cairn Terrier is an accomplished 'begger'. Never teach this trick to a puppy until its back is strong enough to take the strain.

Right: It's anyone's guess what this little Norfolk Terrier puppy is thinking.

Opposite page, bottom: A Skye Terrier on its native Isle of Skye.

Usually black and tan, Welsh Terriers are also allowed to be grizzle. It is usually admitted, even if reluctantly, that there is a cross of Wire Fox Terrier somewhere in their blood. This may have altered the original shape but it has certainly produced a very smart, modern-looking terrier. In its native Wales, the farmers often go out in parties with guns after the hill foxes and the Welsh Terriers accompany them. It is not uncommon for them to be hunted in packs, a rare occurrence with most terriers.

Another native of Wales but a comparative newcomer is the Sealyham Terrier. The breed was founded by Captain John Edwards of the Sealyham estate in about 1860. He aimed to breed a short-legged, strong-jawed, courageous little terrier with a mainly white coat, to be used for badger-digging. How he actually bred

them and from what ingredients no one really knows, but the result was a very smart little dog which soon found favour in the show ring as well as in working circles. The Sealyham's courage was never in doubt, for Captain Edwards used to test the young dogs by setting them to tackle a polecat. The hard white coat served a useful purpose when the dogs were working in bramble thickets, which the soft-coated terriers usually hated. Mostly all white, some Sealyhams have lemon or badger markings on their ears. There are not so many to be seen about now, but they still have a large band of staunch supporters.

A familiar terrier today is the Bull Terrier which has many varieties, all stemming from common ancestry. There are Bull Terriers, Staffordshire Bull Terriers, Miniature Bull Terriers and the

Staffordshire Terrier. Despite its name, the Staffordshire is an all-American product, specifically bred for fighting over 150 years ago. At one time referred to as the Yankee Terrier or Pit Bull Terrier, it finally emerged as the Staffordshire Terrier when dog fighting was tabooed. A larger dog than the Staffordshire Bull, with massive cheek muscles, these tough, tenacious dogs can hold their own with almost anything. The modern descendants of the breed, however, seem no keener on fighting than any other dog and they make affectionate, reliable family guards and are usually excellent with children.

The Staffordshire Bull Terrier, from which the Staffordshire Terrier originated, was also once used for fighting. It became separated from the white terriers, later to be called Bull Terriers, in the mid-nineteenth century. This coloured version did not come to the show ring as soon as the white ones, and it was 1935 before the Kennel Club gave it recognition. By this time dog fighting had become unpopular with public and police alike and the terrier fanciers turned to showing instead. No dog is tougher than the Staffordshire Bull, and it needs careful handling and training if it is to become the asset it should be, and not a liability. If it is allowed to run free, its latent fighting instinct will doubtless be aroused and once it starts fighting nothing will put it off. But the Staffordshire Bull is nevertheless a very trainable dog, some even doing well in working trials and, if treated with respect, it is without peer as a guard of its master's property and children.

The White Bull Terrier, now known as the Bull Terrier, was crossed back to the old coloured variety in the 1920s and it is now just as common to see coloured ones as the all white. Its egg-shaped head, small deep-set eyes, tight-fitting coat and obvious strength, all set in a muscle-packed, sculptured body, make it a dog worth looking at twice. At one time there was a lot of deafness prevalent in the white ones. but this has now been practically bred out. Bull Terriers used to be very popular in

Above: Although increasingly popular as show dogs and pets, most Border Terriers are still tough, game litte dogs.

Top: Although it is not really a good idea to have a dog so near a child's face, this Boston Terrier seems sensible enough.

India, where they withstood the hot climate well. They make excellent guards and companions and are usually good with small children, but, although they are slow to anger, this is not a breed to be trifled with once aroused. The Bull's short white coat is easy to keep well groomed, though it needs very thorough brushing when the dog is casting. A good bath helps to loosen the hairs and let the new coat come through more quickly.

A small variety called the Miniature Bull Terrier is often seen at the larger dog shows. The standard is the same as for its larger cousins but it must weigh under 9 kg (20 lbs) and be under 35 cm (14 ins) high. Not a great number seem to be kept as family pets, but they are neat, loyal little dogs, easy to keep clean, and do not require too much exercise.

Although called a terrier, the Boston Terrier does not really belong to the Terrier Group. In England it is placed in the Utility Group and in America in the Non-sporting Group. An all-American product, needless to say from the region around Boston, this tough, intelligent little dog comes in three sizes – under 6.8 kg (15 lbs), 6.8–9 kg (15–20 lbs) and over 9 kg (20 lbs). They are usually brindle with white markings in a definite pattern, and are compact-bodied, short-coated active dogs with a bright, determined expression, making ideal companions. Originally bred for fighting in the pits, the modern Boston has a less aggressive temperament than its ancestors, but it is an unwise dog which dares to interfere with it, although it does not usually seek out trouble.

The Boston originated from a mixture of breeds, including a fair dose of Bulldog blood, and it is not the easiest of dogs to breed from. Many bitches require caesarian operations in order to deliver their pups safely.

A relative newcomer to the terrier clan is the Australian Terrier. Although produced in Australia and shown there from 1899, it was undoubtedly derived from British exports. Cairns, Dandies, Irish and Yorkshire Terriers were all probably used in the original mixture, and the end result was an agile, compact little dog full of terrier character and pluck, happy to take on rats, snakes or any other vermin. It is a small terrier, weighing about 5 kg (11 lbs) and standing 25 cm (10 ins) high, with a blue or silver coat and tan markings on legs and body, and a straight hard coat. The colour can also be clear sandy or red.

Below: A Lakeland Terrier head study, showing the correct way to trim the dog for show.

Left: The tough little Dandie Dinmont.

Below: A Bull Terrier, made to look even more tough by the patch over one eye.

Right: A working Jack Russell Terrier, out hunting after rabbits.

For anyone wanting a small but sporting terrier, a good town and country dog with a coat that does not show the dirt and is not very difficult to groom, this cheeky, happy little dog has a lot to commend it.

The other native Australian terrier is the Sydney Silkie. Again a mixture of several British breeds, the most-used cross was probably the Australian Terrier and the Yorkshire Terrier. First shown in Sydney in 1907, the new breed was soon being exported to Canada and America where it rapidly became popular. The coat should be flat, glossy and quite long, reaching to the ground, and blue and tan in colour. The Silkie has erect ears, weighs under 4.5 kg (10 lbs) and is a very likable, attractive little dog. But, like the Yorkie, its coat will need a lot of attention and must be kept well groomed.

Although not a registered breed, the Jack Russell Terrier deserves a mention as it has recently become increasingly popular. Years ago a sporting parson from Devonshire had a famous pack of working terriers which became known as 'Parson Jack Russells'. Opinions vary as to what they actually looked like, the probability being that he did not breed them but bought in any terriers which appealed to him in looks and working ability. During the last few decades some owners have become disillusioned over the way fashion has changed some of the old breeds of terriers and have turned to these tough little working types instead. They come long- or short-legged, prick- or drop-eared, short- or broken-coated, usually white with black or tan markings.

Above: An Australian Silkie Terrier is difficult to tell apart from the Yorkshire Terrier, which is one of its ancestors.

Gun Dogs

MAN has used the dog's hunting instinct yet again by developing gun dogs for use in the shooting field. When a wild dog catches its prey, it very often picks it up and carries it back to its den or some other place of safety. This behaviour forms the basis of the retrieving instinct, which has persisted in a lesser or greater degree in the majority of dogs right up to the present day.

The hunting instinct enables a dog to hunt for game in cover often inaccessible to Man, who in any case does not have any 'nose'. But the gun dog must not catch or even pursue its quarry; instead it must stop dead in its tracks and watch its master shoot the prize. This requires a great deal of self-control in the dog, which has to be developed by careful training. Unlike the Greyhound, which is completely out of its handler's control the moment the slips are released, the gun dog must hunt with enthusiasm but still be under restraint, and this is only possible when the submissive instinct is strong enough to balance the hunting instinct.

Gun dogs can be divided into various kinds, used for different jobs in the shooting field. Some flush out the game, some point or set, and others retrieve the shot game. Some modern breeds, noticeably the European gun dogs, have been specially bred as 'pointer/retrievers' and will tackle most jobs involved in the course of shooting.

Gun dogs, as such, have only been in use since the invention of guns and gunpowder. One of the earliest books to describe them was *An Essay on Shooting*, published in 1789. In a chapter on 'Instructions for Training Pointers', the writer (anonymous) says 'there are three species of dog capable of receiving proper instructions and of being trained. These are the Smooth Pointer, the Spaniel and the Rough Pointer. The last is a dog with long curled hair and seems to be a mixed breed of the water dog and the spaniel, but in general is proper only for open country.' Another early gun dog book, Blaine's *Encyclopedia of Rural Sports* published in 1840, tells us that 'the spaniel group includes the Setter, the Common Spaniel, the Newfoundland dog and the Retriever; the whole of which there is much reason to believe are derived from the eastern hunting dogs of scent.'

Depending on what the shooting man of today needs, there is a wide range of gun dogs to choose from. For one or two sportsmen engaged in rough shooting, the best choice is probably a spaniel, such as the large versatile English Springer. But members of a syndicate, where beaters are employed to drive the game, might well have retrievers which wait quietly until given the order to retrieve the shot or wounded birds. Pointers and setters need plenty of open space where they can range out and find the game, indicating its position by coming up on 'point'.

It is often said that the spaniel originated from Spain, but this is by no means certain. There is, however, a nice legend as to how it got its name. When the Carthaginians landed in Spain, the first thing they saw were hundreds of rabbits scurrying from bush to bush. So the soldiers all shouted '*span, span*' which in their language meant 'rabbit'. The country was consequently named Hispania, or Rabbitland, and the dogs used for hunting the rabbits were called spaniels. By the beginning of the nineteenth century, four varieties of spaniel were known, the large and small Water Spaniel and the large and small Land Spaniel. The large Land Spaniel probably became the Field Spaniel and the small one the Cocker Spaniel. In the early 1800s, Lord Rivers spoke of having a well-known strain of black and white 'Cocking Spaniel', the Duke of Norfolk had a larger strain which made 'very good Springers' and the Duke of Newcastle owned a Clumber Spaniel.

At the early dog shows, the spaniel classes were considerably confused and it was not until 1901 that the British Kennel Club began to sort them out into various types. Usually when anyone thinks of a spaniel, it is the little Cocker that springs to mind. Its job in the shooting field is to flush the game from thick cover. It is usually a fast, willing worker, with a very good nose, and can often be taught to retrieve as well. But few Cockers are big enough to lift a large hare and many shooting men prefer the larger Springer. As a companion, if not allowed to indulge its healthy appetites or become lazy, the Cocker is a happy, cheerful little chap always ready to go for a walk or play games. Most are usually very good guards, and some can even be a bit too keen if not kept in check. One drawback of the Cocker as a housedog is its coat, which does bring in mud and dirt and needs a lot of attention if it is not to become matted. But if you are prepared to spend some time and trouble, you will be rewarded with a smart as well as cheerful pet, and you can take your choice of colours as Cockers come in nearly as many colours as the rainbow.

Left: A Large Munsterlander, a German breed which is becoming better known in England.

Right: A Wire-haired Pointing Griffon retrieving. This dual-purpose breed both points and retrieves the game.

The American Cocker varies in several respects from the English Cocker. Both types are shown in both countries and the American Cocker is now making great headway in Britain. The American dog is smaller than the English, has a shorter muzzle and comes in almost as many colours as the English Cocker. It is distinguished by a long, profuse coat which usually touches the ground. These Cockers seem to be very friendly, active little dogs, but not over-renowned for their prowess in the shooting field, where their heavy coat is hardly an asset. It is quite an art to present them well in the show ring and even the pet dog will need a good deal of knowledgeable grooming.

There are also two types of Springer Spaniel, the English and the Welsh. The English has the reputation of being the ideal rough shooter's dog and a good all-rounder. Most are natural retrievers and hunters, like the water, and are tough dogs which take a lot of tiring. They are larger than the Cocker, weighing up to 22 kg (50 lbs), which tends to make them slightly slower in the field. They can be liver and white, liver, tan and white, or black and white, and being fairly high in the leg with not overlong ears do not carry too much

Right: Two alert Brittany Spaniels.

Below: A Welsh Springer Spaniel, trimmed more for show than for work.

Opposite page: English Springer Spaniels eagerly awaiting the command to go into action.

mud around with them. They are still docked, but the working strains usually have more tail left on than the show dogs, the gun dog owner liking to see a bit of 'flag' waving when his dog is working in the field.

The Welsh Springer differs quite a lot from its English cousin. Always a rich red and white, it is smaller and its ears are not so long. It is a strong, active dog, and a very keen worker, although some tend to get rather over-excited. In spite of this, Welsh Springers are very good game-finders with plenty of stamina.

The Clumber Spaniel is rather unlike the other spaniels, more so today than it was 100 years ago. Unfortunately the modern show dogs have become very heavy and big-boned, apt to tire easily when working in rough country. Never a fast worker, the Clumber was at one time very popular in the shooting field; it had a reputation for being very easy to train and for being a good, steady, reliable worker. Before the First World War, these dogs were often trained to work as a team, doing the work that human beaters usually do nowadays. Two of the team would be trained to retrieve, so that when a bird was shot the two chosen would go out on command and fetch back the shot birds, the rest of the team remaining behind. Present-day Clumbers weigh up to 27 kg (60 lbs), with massive heads. They are seldom seen working, which in view of their history is rather a shame. Clumbers have never been very popular as pets, probably because of their rather heavy appearance. Their colouring is white, with occasional lemon markings.

Above: The Irish Water Spaniel is not seen much today, but it is a tough, hard-working dog, especially in the water.

Opposite page, top: The Sussex Spaniel, one of the more rare spaniel breeds today.

Opposite page, bottom: These two Cocker Spaniels seem great friends.

Although popular in the early part of this century, both Sussex and Field Spaniels are now relatively rare. In 1946 only two Sussex Spaniels were registered with the British Kennel Club but their numbers have since picked up again. The Sussex is a unique golden liver colour, a strong, low dog on short sturdy legs. It is a persistent worker and will go into the most formidable cover after game. It would be a pity if this breed should die out, but there are very few in England and even fewer in America.

Field Spaniels are still in favour with some gun dog men as workers, but it is now very difficult to acquire them. Like the Sussex, they are larger spaniels than the Cocker, with a moderately long body and always self-coloured. They lack the panache of the Cocker, especially in the show ring.

The Irish Water Spaniel is rather an odd man out in the spaniel group and not many are seen today, although the breed has a long history as a gun dog. Perhaps more of a retriever than a spaniel, this dog makes an excellent wildfowling dog and comes into its own on the marshes where its oily, curly coat resists the water. This same coat can be rather a hindrance if it is worked in thick cover as it picks up leaves, brambles and other debris. They are known as rather 'hard' dogs and need competent handlers to get the best out of them.

A very attractive spaniel from France which has recently become more popular is the Brittany Spaniel. It is known as a 'pointing spaniel' because it ranges out and then points the sitting birds in the same way as a pointer or setter. Most are orange and white in colour, lightly built with a dense coat and not overmuch feathering. They are moderate-sized, active dogs which make very good companions as well as working dogs.

The retrievers are well known to every sportsman and are equally successful in many other spheres of canine activity. The Labrador and the Golden Retriever are often, for example, used for guiding the blind. A cross between the two breeds is also used and the rejection percentage is low. Both these breeds have made their mark in obedience classes and working trials, and Labradors are frequently used by the police and Customs for drug detection work.

The Labrador is one of the most popular dogs in the shooting field; it responds well, is a good game-finder, a first-rate water dog and a fast and stylish worker. Its short water-resistant coat has many advantages for the pet owner and many Labradors often make good guard dogs. The Labrador came to Britain in the mid-nineteenth century, arriving on the Newfoundland fishing boats bringing cod to Poole harbour. In 1840, in his book *The Moor and the Loch*, John Colquhoun tells of a retriever which would go back a great distance to pick up its master's whip if it had been accidentally dropped, and on another occasion picked up a shawl which had fallen from an open carriage and tenderly brought it back. So apparently retrievers were just as versatile then as they are today.

Opposite page: Although the Clumber Spaniel naturally looks sad, most are tenacious workers.

Left: The Labrador Retriever has been used for many other jobs besides retrieving. Police forces throughout the world use them as 'sniffer dogs' to detect drugs and explosives.

Below: A Labrador employed at its traditional work of retrieving game.

The Golden Retriever is popular both as a working and a show dog, and many prize-winners work with enthusiasm in the shooting field. Golden Retrievers were first exhibited in 1908, but their origin is uncertain. They are handsome dogs, with good noses, kind temperaments and a ready acceptance of training. The Golden Retriever carries more coat than the Labrador, with feathering on legs and tail, but most owners feel that the satisfaction of owning such an attractive and sensible companion is well worth any extra time spent caring for it.

The Curly-coated and the Flat-coated Retrievers are not so well known, although the Flat-coat was used extensively at the large shoots held in the early part of this century. First shown in 1870, Flat-coats were then called Wavy-coats, but the wave was discouraged and they are now universally known as Flat-coats. At one stage a Borzoi cross was introduced into the breed, resulting in completely foreign heads, but by careful breeding this has now almost been eliminated. The Flat-coats are medium-sized, very active dogs, black or liver in colour, and easy to train and handle.

Although kept by many gamekeepers of 50 years ago, not many Curly-coated Retrievers are seen today. They are tough dogs, not among the easiest to train and not averse to having a go at a poacher as well as retrieving shot game! Good dogs in the water, some tend to be scatterbrained but they make up for this with a tremendous amount of courage. Like the Flat-coat, they can be black or liver-coloured and their coat should be a mass of crisp curls all over.

The Chesapeake Bay Retriever is an American breed which originated in 1807 when two puppies, said to be from Newfoundland, were shipwrecked off the coast of Maryland. Both proved to be first-class water dogs and were mated with local gun dogs to start the Chesapeake strain. Although not very popular with dog show enthusiasts, the Chesapeake is a regular participator in American field trials. Not many are seen in Britain, perhaps because the native retriever breeds have proved more than adequate for the work required of them.

Last of the gun dogs are the setters and pointers, which are required to range out over open country, find the game and then 'point' or 'set' to indicate its position to the following guns. In America pointers and setters are also expected to retrieve the shot game, but in Britain they are usually restricted to their original work of pointing, as it is felt that it tends to make them unsteady if they are taught to retrieve as well. The show and working types of setters are very different.

The handsome English Setter, the flashy Red Irish Setter and the workman-like black-and-tan Gordon Setter from Scotland were all originally 'setting spaniels' until gradually, by selective breeding, the different types emerged.

The English Setter is a beautiful animal with a soft, silky coat, feathered tail and attractive colouring. Slightly smaller than the other setters, it makes a decorative and easily trainable companion. In America, where they are very popular as working dogs, a small strain has been developed solely for trials.

With its rich red coat and handsome good looks, it is not surprising that the Irish Setter classes at the dog shows are well filled and that it is also a popular family dog. It should nevertheless be remembered that these are dogs bred for ranging over open country and that they do not take kindly to being kept on a leash in town. The Irish Setter has a reputation for being rather headstrong, so if you should decide to own one bear this in mind and be prepared to spend time on training and exercise. When worked in field trials, it usually has a good nose and a wide range but it can be a little unpredictable.

The Gordon is the largest of the setters, a big, handsome fellow, jet black with bright chestnut markings. Believed to have been bred by the Duke of Richmond and Gordon in 1827, both Bloodhound and Collie crosses are rumoured to have been included in its genealogy. Gordons first reached the show ring in 1859. They are very strong, well-built dogs, not quite as fast as the other two setters but good stayers and persistent workers. They are usually very trainable and make good companions and family dogs.

The classic image of a pointer is of a dog standing still as a statue, head and nose lifted on outstretched neck, one foreleg lifted, tail stiff and straight, the whole animal the epitome of concentration. Largely because of changing times and the encroachment of towns into the countryside, not so many pointers are now used in the shooting field in Britain, although the show classes are very well filled. Many years ago the Spanish Pointer was imported to Britain and today's pointers are probably bred from this stock. They are normally highly strung, like most bird dogs, but at the same time stylish workers and fascinating to watch.

More recently, several other pointers have been introduced to Britain, America and Australia. The Vizsla hails from Hungary, and the Weimaraner, the German Short-haired and the German Wire-haired Pointers from Germany. The German Wire-haired is not so well known outside its

Opposite page: Irish Setters always catch the eye with their beautiful bright chestnut coats.

Above: A working-type English Setter, not as glamorous as the show type but an attractive working dog.

native country but is becoming increasingly recognized in Canada and America. These breeds are all-purpose gun dogs, being expected to find the game, point it and then retrieve it when shot. A tall order for one dog but many manage very well, even if they do not have the style and expertise of the specialists.

The Vizsla was specially bred for the shooting field in Hungary, even down to its sandy yellow coat which fits in so well with the Hungarian countryside. It is a strongly built, smooth-coated dog, perhaps a trifle self-willed but nevertheless a good sporting dog.

The Weimaraner is sometimes confused with the Vizsla, although it is always a silver grey colour, earning it the nickname of the 'grey ghost'. Used originally for tracking game, it was later trained for pointing and retrieving and quickly adapted to its new role. These dogs have been used by police forces and are sometimes also seen in obedience and working trials where they give a very good account of themselves.

Dating back to the early nineteenth century, the German Short-Haired Pointer is now well known the world over as a dual-purpose gun dog. It is believed to have both Spanish and English Pointer blood in its veins. These are clean-cut, smooth-coated dogs, popular with both sportsman and exhibitor alike. A number of show-winners work in the shooting field, and to become a full champion in England a dog must also win certain qualifications in field trials.

The German Wire-haired Pointer is very like the short-haired version to look at, except that instead of a smooth coat it has a harsh, wiry coat.

Below: A Weimaraner, a dual-purpose German gun dog, making light work of carrying a rabbit.

Right: A Golden Retriever retrieving a pheasant.

Middle right: A German Wire-haired Pointer is an excellent companion in the field.

Bottom right: A German Short-haired Pointer in a classic pose 'on point'.

Herding Dogs

BY the time Man started to domesticate animals such as the horse, cow and sheep, the dog must have been well established as an aid to hunting and probably as a guard dog. But the hunting dog would have been of little use to the farmer who kept sheep or cattle, and indeed it might well have killed them. On the other hand, a dog which would help round up other domestic animals without attacking them would have been a great asset. And so the herding breeds were developed from the dogs which were already there – the hunting breeds.

The herding instinct is only a slight variation of the hunting instinct and it was probably not very difficult to develop one from the other. In any hunting pack there are dogs which will run round the quarry and turn it back into the pack. By breeding from these dogs, one could produce dogs with a natural instinct to run round other animals. It was also vital that these dogs should not kill their quarry. Working sheepdogs still retain their instinct to hunt and kill and the reason they do not do so when working is because they are trained, and they can only be trained provided the submissive instinct is strong enough to counter-balance the very strong hunting instinct. In developing the herding breeds, Man has therefore bred for a strong submissive instinct. Generally speaking, dogs from the herding breeds are more easily trained than those from the hound and terrier groups.

Some breeds classified as sheepdogs are not, in fact, herding breeds at all. They are really guard dogs and are only called sheepdogs because they have been used to guard sheep. They usually originated in parts of the world where flocks needed to be protected against predators such as wolves and bears, even humans. There are also sheepdog breeds which have been used as guard dogs without any particular association with sheep.

In some countries, particularly on the Continent, sheepdogs have been produced which both herd and guard the flocks. It is the practice to 'fold' sheep in enclosures of hurdles or netting, which are moved on to fresh ground each day. For this type of work, the dog has to be 'close-run' and noisy – a driver rather than a true herder. The British shepherd, unlike his European counterpart, has not needed to keep dogs which could tackle a wolf for several

centuries and he does not need to bring his sheep into enclosed areas every night for protection. The sheep are simply left to roam the hills day and night. But when he does want to gather them in, he requires a very different sort of dog from that needed in most other parts of the world. He needs a true herding dog and it was in Britain that this type of dog originated, and from Britain spread to most countries in the New World.

At one time, practically all sheep in the south of England were kept in folds. This was not for protection, but because more sheep could be kept by cultivating crops like turnips and kale and grazing them with sheep in a controlled manner. The shepherd's dog was very like the Old English Sheepdog, and it was also the drover's dog and the cow dog on the dairy farm. On top of these duties, it was also expected to be a good guard dog. It has always been the custom to dock this breed very short and the Old English Sheepdog is often referred to as the Bobtail. In winter the Bobtail spent most of its time working in mud, when one would expect its enormous coat to be a hindrance, but it should be remembered that working dogs never develop the heavy coats of the show dogs. It was also the general practice to shear the dogs at the same time as the sheep, and even to dip them.

As folded sheep were replaced by grassland sheep, so the Old English Sheepdog declined as a worker. It was, however, crossed with the Border Collie which came from Scotland, and we find local strains like the Dorset Blue Shag and the Smithfield Dog of East Anglia. The latter was a favourite with drovers in the days when sheep and cattle were driven to London's Smithfield Market.

Left: A small Hungarian cattle dog demonstrating the herding dog's capacity to 'heel'.

Right, above: A windswept group of Bearded Collies. The colour of the 'odd man out' is permitted in the standard.

Right, below: The Old English Sheepdog has a lot in common with the Beardies above, but it is larger and heavier-coated.

As the Old English Sheepdog's use as a working dog declined, its popularity as a pet and show dog increased. This breed has become particularly popular in America and in many other countries where dog shows are common. It is an intelligent, active dog, very trainable and an excellent guard. But it should also be remembered that it is really quite big and boisterous, especially when young, and it has an enormous coat, now cultivated to such an extent that it looks almost more like a sheep than a sheepdog.

Scotland also has a shaggy sheepdog, the Bearded Collie, and superficially its appearance is similar to the Bobtail. It has the same heavy coat, though not so long, but the tail is left on, giving the dog a somewhat different outline. Like the Bobtail, the Beardie is a 'close-run' dog and

a very noisy worker favoured by drovers and farmers, but it was never very popular with shepherds because its coat 'balled' in the snow. The half-Beardie – a mixture of Border Collie and Beardie – is also very popular in some areas. Several attempts were made to popularize the Bearded Collie as a show dog, but it was not until 1948 that the breed was recognized by the British Kennel Club. Since then it has become quite numerous on the Continent and in Scandinavia. As a worker it is much in favour in New Zealand and there are far more Bearded Collies working there today than in Scotland.

As a companion, the Beardie is similar in many ways to the Bobtail. It is intelligent, affectionate, very active in both mind and body, and requires plenty of exercise. Like most of the herding breeds,

Below: If you like Collies but not the long coat, the Smooth Collie has the same shape but a less troublesome coat to look after.

Opposite page: This handsome Rough Collie would make a beautiful pet.

the Beardie can be easily trained and is normally a good guard dog. Though long, its coat is not curly or woolly and therefore does not carry as much mud as one might expect. It is much easier to groom than the dense coats of the Bobtail or Poodle.

Another breed of shaggy sheepdog native to Britain is the little-heard-of Old Welsh Grey. This is very similar in appearance and style of working to the Bearded Collie, and it is possible that these two breeds and the Old English Sheepdog have common ancestry, although history does not tell us nearly as much about the herding breeds as it does about the hunting dogs.

The Collie is believed to have existed in its present form since very early times; it has been said that the rough-coated ones were bred in the Highlands of Scotland where they needed their coats as a protection against the cold, and that the smooth-coats were used by drovers in the Scottish Lowlands. But working dogs are bred for working ability rather than type, and Nature has been left to develop the type best suited to the purpose. The result is that there are many different types of Collie, which nevertheless are all pure-bred Collies.

One of the first breeds of dog to achieve fame as a show dog was a Collie. In 1860 Queen Victoria bought a very handsome dog when on a visit to Balmoral, and it subsequently became one of her favourite breeds. Royal patronage almost invariably draws public attention to a breed and the Collie quickly became popular both as a companion and a show dog. It was first shown in 1861 as a 'Scotch sheep dog' and in

1881 the Collie Club was formed. To say the breed became popular is something of an understatement, as in the 1880s several dogs were sold for prices varying from £500 to £1,500 and in those days one could buy a fair-sized farm for that amount. This breed is now officially known as the Rough Collie, but also unofficially as the Show Collie or the 'Lassie Collie' because of its association with the M.G.M. film star Lassie. Today the Rough Collie, either in its original form or its modern show type, is rarely seen as a working dog, but it is very popular as a show dog and companion. Many people regard it as one of the most handsome dogs and it is not too difficult to keep it looking well. Although heavy-coated, there is only slight feathering on the forelegs, while the hindlegs are quite smooth to the hocks. The coat is straight and harsh, so that mud does not cling to it as readily as with some other breeds.

There is also a Smooth Collie, identical to the Rough apart from its coat. Admirers of the breed claim that it is more beautiful than the Rough as one can see and admire its graceful outlines. It is a very clean dog to keep in the house, but it has never become as popular as its Rough cousin.

Many other types of Collie have been used in the hill sheepfarming areas of Scotland, England and Wales for centuries. One dog can do the work of ten men – and do it better – and the high cost of labour has made the dog more valuable today than ever before.

In recent years the breeding and training of sheepdogs has become much more scientific and sophisticated. Sheepdog trials have had much to do with this and

have resulted in a specialist dog bred for the purpose, now known generally as the Border Collie. Because the first sheepdog trial was held in Bala in North Wales in 1873, and because trials have been popular in Wales ever since, many people think the Border Collie is of Welsh origin and even refer to it as the Welsh Sheepdog. But at that very first trial it was a Scotsman with a Scottish-bred dog who won the championship, starting a big boom in the export of dogs from Scotland to Wales and, as a result, the native Welsh Sheepdog has become practically extinct.

The Border Collie derives its name from the border between Scotland and England, but it is a name only used in recent times. The International Sheepdog Society, founded in 1906, refers to it as a working sheepdog, and the stud book has sections for rough-coated, smooth-coated and beardie-coated. In Scotland it is also called the 'trial-bred dog' or 'creeper', a most apt name for describing its style of working. It is the style of working, rather than its appearance, which makes this dog different from all other breeds and types of sheepdog. The Border Collie has what is known as 'strong eye', enabling it to 'hold' a single sheep with its 'eye'. What it does, in fact, is to creep steadily and stealthily towards its 'prey', never for an instant relaxing its menacing stare. The sheep becomes almost mesmerized and either stands still or moves backwards. The 'eye' is so strong that it even affects people.

Dogs cannot be taught to work in this way, they must be bred to do it. The 'strong eye' is merely an exaggeration of the wild dog's natural instinct to stalk its prey. Until

Opposite page: Sheepdogs at work. The one on the left is a 'strong-eyed dog', showing the style of working which has made the Border Collie supreme for trial work and for some of the work on a sheep farm. The 'loose-eyed dog' standing up at the back is more of an all-rounder.

Above: The Swedish Valhund has a lot in common with the Welsh Corgi.

Right: A Pembroke Corgi playing with her puppy.

they are trained, the majority of good young dogs follow that instinct a stage further by grabbing hold of the sheep, but as their submissive instinct is also very highly developed it is not usually very difficult to teach them not to do this. The attitude adopted by the strong-eyed sheepdog is exactly the same as that adopted by pointers and setters, and a sheepdog will set at a sheep which it scents but cannot see, for example, a sheep buried in snow, just as a bird dog sets at a grouse.

'Strong eye' is by no means the only quality of the modern Border Collie. It is a wide-running, stylish worker which, when handled properly, can surpass any other type of sheepdog for certain types of work. But, because it is such a high-powered dog, it does require very delicate handling. Bred carefully, the herding instinct in the Border Collie can only be described as over-developed. It will literally work, or try to work, anything from a mouse to an elephant. Contrary to common belief, sheepdogs do not learn to work by watching other dogs or by being taught by their owners. They 'run' instinctively and it is up to the owner to teach them how, when and where to run.

The Border Collie has found its way to every country in the world where sheep are herded. Sheepdog trials are held in Australia, New Zealand, North and South America, Africa and many other countries. In recent years the breed has also become very popular and successful in obedience competitions. A dog so completely obsessed with work as the majority of Border Collies are will quickly become neurotic if denied any outlet for this instinct. When the

submissive instinct is equally strong, the dog will try to do anything its trainer asks of it, which is why the breed is so successful in the obedience ring. Without training and adequate exercise, the Border Collie is one of the most unsuitable of all dogs to keep as a pet.

At present the Border Collie is not recognized by the British Kennel Club or shown at dog shows, although it is shown in Australia. It is a difficult breed for which to set a standard of points, as there is a wide variation in size, with some smooth, some rough and some 'in-between' coats. The predominant colour is black and white, followed by black and tan and white, but one also finds dogs which are nearly all black or nearly all white, as well as chocolates, sables and blue merles.

The Welsh Corgi is another British herding breed which was made popular by royal patronage. Although known to be a very old breed, there seems to be no conclusive evidence as to where it originated. It is essentially a cattle dog and, although it will work sheep, it is much too rough and inclined to 'heel'.

There are two types of Corgi: the Pembroke and the Cardigan. The most obvious difference between the two is that the former has a short tail and the latter a long tail. The 'Cardi' is altogether a bigger dog, in a wider variety of colours. It has a less 'foxy' head and its forelegs are slightly bowed. The Corgi was first recognized by the Kennel Club in 1925 but it was not until 1934 that the two breeds were separated. Until then docking was prohibited and, although most Pembrokes were born with short tails, they varied in length from half

tails to no tails at all, presenting rather an untidy spectacle in the show ring. Since docking has been allowed, their appearance has become more uniform, but the percentage of natural short tails has decreased until it is quite unusual to find a natural bob-tailed puppy.

In 1934 the already popular Corgis were given a great boost when the Duke of York bought a Pembroke Corgi puppy for Princess Elizabeth, now Queen Elizabeth II. From then on the Pembroke Corgi quickly rose in popularity and for several years it was one of the top registered dogs in Britain. The Cardigan Corgi has never become as popular, either because it never had the good fortune to be patronized by royalty or because most people prefer the rather smarter, smaller Pembroke Corgi. Corgis also became popular overseas and were exported to America, Canada, New Zealand, Australia, South Africa and most European countries. Though not quite so much in favour today, the breed still ranks as one of the most popular show dog breeds in the world. In comparison with many other breeds, the show Corgi is hardly any different to its working cousin, and the shape of the head in particular has not changed at all.

As a pet the Corgi has many virtues and quite a few faults. It is a very game and gay little dog, with characteristics falling somewhere between the sheepdogs and the terriers. It is very intelligent but not always anxious to please, and its worst fault is a tendency to be over-excitable and noisy. The old heeling instinct very often comes to the surface and the human Achilles tendon seems to make a very good substitute for a cow's heel! Fortunately the show strains of today have much less inclination to do this than the original Corgis which came from the Welsh hills fifty years ago. It is one of those instincts which should be nipped in the bud very quickly. Generally speaking, the Cardigan has a steadier, less excitable temperament than the Pembroke.

A couple of other breeds bear a remarkable resemblance to the Corgi: the Lancashire Heeler of Britain, a very localized breed rarely seen outside its native county, and the Swedish Valhund, so closely resembling a Pembroke Corgi that one feels sure they must have common ancestry. Some say the Vikings stole the Corgis from Wales and took them back to Scandinavia, and some say that the Corgi came to Wales with the Vikings. The Welsh believe that Corgis have always existed in Wales and many legends surround the breed.

As its name implies, the Shetland Sheepdog is native to the group of islands off the north coast of Scotland. There seems to be little information on the history of the breed. It has been said that the reason why Shetland ponies, cattle sheep and dogs are small is because larger animals could not live under the rigorous conditions on the Islands, but while this is probably true of the herbivores it would not apply to dogs which do not live directly off the land. Small sheepdogs have existed in the Shetlands for as long as anyone can remember, and when tourists started going there they brought these pretty little dogs back with them. At Crufts Dog Show in 1906 several were exhibited and the breed was recognized by the British Kennel Club in

1909, although there was much dispute as to which was the correct type. The native Shetland Sheepdogs were not much like the ones seen in the ring today; they looked more like miniature Border Collies and are still to be found working in the Islands today. They had broad heads, well-defined stops, bold friendly eyes and were smaller than the average show ring specimen. Some breeders agreed, quite reasonably, that as this was the type to be found in the Shetlands it was the type which should be maintained, but others argued that the breed should resemble as closely as possible a miniature show ring Rough Collie. The latter opinion won the day and the Shetland Sheepdog of today looks very much like a miniature Rough Collie.

The breed is popular in most countries both as a show and pet dog. It is very pretty, easy to keep looking well and of course eats less than the larger sheepdogs. It is very intelligent and easy to train but it is a sensitive breed and some are very nervous. But if you take care to choose one with a good temperament, the Sheltie is a charming little dog to own.

With the Border Collie, the Kelpie is one of the two most important breeds of working sheepdog in the world today. But unlike its British ancestor, the Kelpie seems to have stayed in its native Australia where it has proved its value on the great sheep stations. It is estimated that some 80,000 of the breed are currently working in Australia.

Not surprisingly, Australia's first sheepdogs came from Scotland. In 1870 a pair of Scottish sheepdogs produced a puppy called Gleeson's Kelpie which, mated

to Caesar, also bred from imported stock, produced King's Kelpie which won Australia's first sheepdog trial in 1872. It is believed that all Kelpies are descended from that one bitch, but there is some difference of opinion as to what other ingredients went into the creation of the breed. Some people say that Dingo blood was introduced, pointing to the Kelpie's prick ears and smooth coat as evidence. But there always have been, and still are, sheepdogs in Scotland and Wales which have prick ears and smooth coats. The most likely answer is that the Australian ingredients went into the creation of the stock to evolve their own sheepdog to work under their own conditions. They needed a dog which could work sheep in thousands rather than hundreds, as in Britain, and they ended up with a tough, independent working dog, very wide-running and showing as much 'eye' as a good Border Collie.

There are classes for the breed at Australian dog shows and some are kept as pets, but it will always be on the huge sheep stations that the breed really comes into its own, doing the work it was bred for and at which it excels.

The Australian Cattle Dog came into existence at about the same time as the Kelpie and no doubt with much of the same ancestry. In this case, however, it seems to be generally agreed that Dingo blood *was* used to add toughness to the already tough Scottish stock. Dogs had worked cattle in Britain long before Australia was discovered, but 100 head of cattle was considered quite a big drove and there were hedges and ditches round the fields and

Right: A large number of Alsatians, or German Shepherd Dogs, are trained for obedience work.

Opposite page: An Australian Kelpie 'backing' sheep in a truck. If there is no room for the dog to get round the side of the sheep to bring them out of a truck or sheep pen, then it must go over their backs.

along the old drove roads. In New South Wales and Victoria a 'mob' of cattle can be over 1,000 head, while the 'paddocks' can run into thousands of acres. The cattle are controlled by dogs working alongside mounted 'jackaroos', or cowboys. Weaklings have no place in this type of farming and, just to be able to survive, dogs need to be really tough. Explicit commands cannot be given in the same way as they are with a dog working at a sheepdog trial or on a quiet hillside in Wales or Scotland, so the Cattle Dog has to be able to think for itself and use its own initiative. The result is an extremely intelligent animal with exceptional agility of both mind and body.

The breed is remarkably true to type, with a head very similar to that of the Welsh Corgi. It has been popular in Australia as a show dog since about 1936, but does not seem to have attracted much attention outside its native country.

Perhaps the best known of all the herding breeds is the Alsatian or German Shepherd Dog, but today it is far better known as a police dog, guard dog, guide dog for the blind or family pet than as a sheepdog. The Alsatian, however, is essentially a sheepdog breed and trials are held for it in its native country. Sheep are kept under the folding system on the Continent, so the trials are very different and the German Shepherd would stand little chance in a British-style sheepdog trial, just as the Border Collie would be pretty hopeless in a trial run under German rules.

The Alsatian is a very old breed and has been used to herd and guard flocks for as long as anyone seems to remember. In a country where wolves are not unknown, even today, it was necessary to have a larger, stronger dog than the sheepdogs of Britain. The breed first attracted attention during World War I when Alsatians were used extensively by the German Army as messenger dogs, patrol dogs, Red Cross dogs, and so on. At the beginning of hostilities in 1914, when the British authorities had never thought of using dogs in war, the Germans had 60,000 dogs already trained. Most of these were German Shepherds, a breed physically as well as mentally suited for the job. During the War, soldiers from many countries came in contact with the breed, realized its abilities and took the dogs home with them. A puppy from a litter found in a dug-out in France was taken to America and became Rin-tin-tin, the first great canine film star.

Because of the War, the name German Shepherd Dog was not very popular in Britain and so the breed was renamed the Alsatian Wolfdog, Alsatian because the dogs which were brought to Britain came from Alsace. Wolfdog was subsequently dropped from the name and the breed became officially known first as the Alsatian and then as the Alsatian (German Shepherd Dog).

By 1926 the breed had the highest number of registrations in both Britain and America, but many dogs unfortunately got into the wrong hands and earned themselves a bad reputation. Many of the breed do have a nervous trait in their make-up and a nervous dog the size of a German Shepherd is a dangerous dog. It is essentially a working dog and can become very frustrated if given nothing to do. As a result, there have been many tragic cases of

children being badly mauled or even killed by dogs not under proper control. This is very unfortunate as, given correct handling, a good German Shepherd is a very good dog indeed. No dog breed has ever suffered so much from adverse publicity and the numbers dropped rapidly. Australia put a complete ban on imports of Alsatians on the grounds that they worried sheep, and this ban has only now been partially lifted. But in spite of all that was said against it, the breed retained a strong band of staunch supporters and has today come back into favour again, though more quietly.

During World War II, the breed again served with armies on both sides, not only as a guard and patrol dog but also as a mine detector and First Aid dog. One of its tasks as a First Aid dog was to go out looking for wounded soldiers in the battle zones, carrying with it medical equipment. Members of the breed have proved most successful as guide dogs for the blind and, of course, everyone knows how successful they have been as police dogs. What must be remembered is that the dog which arrests an armed criminal today may be searching for a lost infant tomorrow, and in most civilized countries the first essential of a police dog is that it does not bite unnecessarily.

No other breed can equal the German Shepherd Dog for versatility and one reason for this is its convenient size. It is a big dog, but not too big, with a close, weather-resistant coat which requires the minimum of attention. The German Shepherd does not shiver like a Boxer or a Doberman when out on a wet, cold night with a policeman on the beat.

Quite a few members of the breed have long coats, but these are regarded as a fault in the show ring and there is no separate recognition for long-coated specimens as there is with Rough and Smooth Collies.

In Holland and Belgium there are sheepdogs with a strong likeness to the German Shepherd and it would appear that at one time they all had common ancestors. One example is the Dutch Herder which is very popular in its native country, but has never become very well known outside Holland. It is divided into three breeds: rough-coated, long-coated and smooth-coated. It is still used as a sheepdog, cattle dog and guard dog and appears to be a good all-rounder. The predominant colour is grey, in various shades from very light to nearly black.

Belgian sheepdogs are similar in type to the Dutch Herder and have become quite well known outside Belgium, particularly in America. Best known is the long-haired, black variety established from old working stock by a M. Rose of Groenendael in 1880 and consequently named the Groenendael. In Belgium it was recognized as a breed in 1891 and soon became popular in both France and Holland. The breed first came to Britain from France in 1931 but was little heard of before the Second World War. After the War it became steadily better known and the Belgian Shepherd Dog Association of Great Britain was formed in 1965.

Slightly lighter in build than the German Shepherd Dog, the Groenendael is used in Europe as a police, sheep and cattle dog as well as for many other purposes. In America and Britain it has proved equally

Opposite page, above: An Alsatian (German Shepherd Dog) with its police handler in Florida.

Opposite page, below: A police Alsatian being worked on a long lead so that it will not be confused by the scent of its handler.

Above: Samoyeds are popular members of the Spitz family.

popular as a worker, companion and in the show ring. Given the opportunity, this Belgian Sheepdog could be expected to carry out any of the tasks usually allotted to the German Shepherd.

The Belgian Tervuren was established by breeders near the Tervuren and is to all intents and purposes a fawn-coloured Groenendael. Indeed the first Tervuren champion in 1907 was by the black Piccard D'Uccle, the foundation sire of the Groenendael. In many countries the two breeds are still shown in the same classes as Belgian Sheepdogs. Tervurens have only recently come to Britain where they are still shown under the classification of a Rare Breed. As a worker and companion, the Tervuren is no different from the Groenendael and one day it may well catch up with its black brother in popularity.

A popular French sheepdog is the Briard, one of the many herding breeds which have also been used for a long time as guard dogs. The Briard is a very well-established breed dating back to the twelfth century, and it is believed that Emperor Charlemagne gave pairs of Briards as gifts to his friends. The breed was also a favourite with Napoleon, who took them on his expedition to Egypt and had several with him in exile in Corsica.

There is so much similarity between the Briard, the Old English Sheepdog and the Bearded Collie, both in appearance and behaviour, that it seems likely that there is a connection between the three breeds. The Briard is larger than either of the other two and is used in its native country as a police dog as well as for working with sheep and cattle. It was also used successfully by the French Army in both World Wars. Apart from the usual duties of patrol dog, messenger dog and so on, the breed was found to be strong enough to carry ammunition and equipment on a specially made pack saddle.

The Briard has been popular in Canada and America since the 1920s but has only recently become known in Britain, although its popularity is increasing rapidly. It is a very active breed, both physically and mentally, and has a surprising turn of speed. It is a natural guard and is often suspicious of strangers. Some, unfortunately, are actually afraid of strangers and if you are considering buying one, you should be careful to select a puppy from stock which is not nervous. Apart from this, it is a most affectionate dog, responsive and easy to train. For some unknown reason, the breed standard insists on double dew claws behind and these can cause trouble if not kept well trimmed and can even grow right back into the leg, causing a very painful sore. The long, slightly wavy coat needs daily attention if it is to look as beautiful as it should. If it is not kept well groomed, mats can form, causing a lot of unnecessary discomfort to the dog when you do have to remove them and, if left for too long, eventually ruining the coat.

Another European breed only recently imported to Britain is the Bouvier de Flandres. 'Bouvier' means cowherd or drover, and although there are a number of cattle dogs in the Low Countries the Bouvier de Flandres has always been very popular with cattle men. However, since modern farming methods took over and cattle have been transported by road and rail, rather than driven along the roads, this breed has been less in demand as a working dog. But this has been remedied to a certain extent by the fact that it has become quite well known as a show dog, especially in Canada and America. It is also often trained for working trials and police work. Rather like a Giant Schnauzer in appearance, this is a tough, rugged-looking dog, muscular and cobby, with a rough wiry coat. Kept under proper control, it is a determined guard dog.

Further south, and found on both the French and Spanish sides of the Pyrenees, is the home of the Pyrenean Mountain Dog, known as Great Pyrenees in America. This impressive dog, massive in size with a thick, warm white or nearly white jacket, was specially bred centuries ago to guard the flocks from wolves and bears. It needed to be able to work day and night 1,500 m (5,000 ft) up in the mountains and is consequently extremely hardy. It is doubtful if Pyrenean Mountain Dogs ever worked the flocks as sheepdogs, their main duty being to guard them. The smaller Pyrenean Sheepdog, with a shorter coat and more agile, was used alongside them for the actual herding.

Not surprisingly, this handsome, dignified dog has become popular all over the world as a show dog and companion. If you intend to own one, remember the thick coat needs a lot of attention and tends to leave white hairs on the carpets. This breed also needs plenty of space and plenty of food – many of them weigh over 45 kg (100 lbs). The Pyrenean Mountain Dog is very independent and a superb guard, often a little too keen for the conditions under which we expect it to live today. We knew of one massive dog which travelled on the back seat of the car when out with its attractive young female owner. All was well if her passenger was another girl. But let her dare to take a boyfriend with her, and sooner or later a huge paw was thrust between them and the poor chap felt heavy breathing down his neck and heard a warning growl in his ear. Only doing what it considered its duty, the poor dog had to find another home as its owner got a little tired of finding new boyfriends!

From Hungary comes another handsome all-white dog, possibly an ancestor of the Pyrenean. The Kuvasz has been known for some time in the American show ring but has only recently been seen at British dog shows. Its name comes from the Turkish word 'kawasw', meaning 'guardian of nobles', and it has been used for well over 1,000 years to guard the flocks of sheep and cattle herded on the great Hungarian steppes. Today it is now used mainly in its native country as a guard dog on farms and estates. The Kuvasz is a very keen, ardent guard and at one time it was common to see it with heavy logs attached to its collar as a precaution to keep it within the boundaries of the farm. Strangers stood little chance of escaping unharmed if one of these dogs was on patrol.

Two more Hungarian herding breeds are the Komondor and the Puli, both of which are also very ancient breeds. A legend about the Komondor tells how a tenth-century Serb shepherd found a litter of wolf cubs. He killed those which sipped, wolf-fashion, but gave those which lapped, dog-fashion, to the village women to bring up. In due course they were crossed with

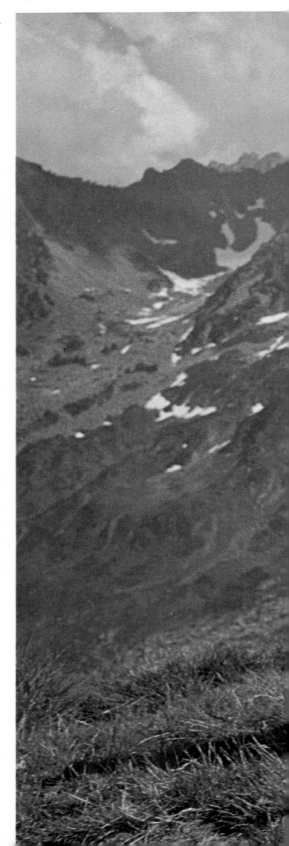

Right: The Briard, an attractive old French sheepdog breed, can still be seen working in France, although not in England.

Below: A Pyrenean Mountain Dog in its home setting. Compared with the show dogs on page 125 this dog has an altogether more workmanlike appearance.

local dogs and the result was the Komondor. The Hungarian sheep live semi-wild out on the bleak Hungarian steppes for four or five months of the year and the Komondor has no equal at herding these timid sheep quietly and competently.

Both the Komondor and the Puli have extraordinary coats. Long and extremely dense, their coats form into cords – in working conditions, felty mats – making them ideal for the constant exposure to harsh weather conditions they have to withstand when they are out with the sheep. Show dogs, of course, do not have the mats but the cords are carefully cultivated and the dogs can be washed without disturbing them. The Komondor is always white, but the smaller Puli is usually reddish-black or grey. Pulis have traditionally worked nearer the villages and

consequently seem to have adapted to town life quite happily, making good companions and house guards.

Another large, mainly white sheep dog, obviously a close relation of both the Pyrenean and the Kuvasz, is the Maremma from the central plains of Italy. Slightly smaller and lighter in build than the Pyrenean, this breed has never become very popular in other countries although a few are seen in England and at the larger dog shows. The Maremma is a tough, hardy breed, as would be expected from its history; used for guarding the flocks against wolves, bears and human thieves, the dogs would stay out day and night in all weather, their food consisting mainly of curds and whey and a sort of mealy porridge. They make excellent, and decorative, guards on large estates for they have a strong territorial

instinct. We have known several which
when first let out in the morning would do
a complete tour of the whole property
completely on their own. Being satisfied
that all was well, they would then come
back and lie calmy, but watchfully, by the
gate.

Portugal has several rather attractive
herding breeds, most of which are dual-
purpose dogs, inasmuch as that they are
also used as guard dogs. As a rule, cattle
dogs are rather on the small side, but in
countries where they were required to
defend the flocks from wolves and bears
they were usually larger. Two of the better-
known Portuguese breeds are the Estrella
Mountain Dog, formerly known as the
Portuguese Mountain Dog, and the
Portuguese Sheepdog. Both are exhibited in
their own country and are gradually

becoming known elsewhere. The first
Estrella Mountain Dogs came to Britain in
1974. They are heavily built dogs, weighing
up to 45 kg (100 lbs), with a soft, medium-
length coat in a variety of colours, and a
sensible broad head with a well-defined
stop. The Estrella is a hardy, independent
breed which still retains its keen guarding
instinct, and in Portugal was often used
rather like a small horse to draw carts
carrying wine or cork.

The Portuguese Sheepdogs are bright,
lively dogs, not as large as the Mountain
Dogs but originally used for the same
purpose. They have fairly long hair with
whiskers and eyebrows and come in a
variety of colours from fawn to black; there
is also a smooth variety. They are now
quite rare even in their own country and
they are not yet shown outside Portugal.

**Opposite page: The Puli is not to
everyone's taste, but if you can cope
with the unusual coat these dogs have
a lot of character.**

**Above: Like the Puli, the Komondor is
a working dog from Hungary. Its coat
is a mass of weather-resistant cords
which hang down over its body.**

Apart from the German Shepherd Dog, Germany has produced several other well-known breeds of what could be termed 'general utility dogs' – dogs that will help with the cattle, make good companions or equally good police dogs. Some are of ancient lineage, others of more recent 'manufacture'.

The Rottweiler is one of the more ancient breeds, taking its name from the town of Rottweil in southern Germany. Many years ago it was called the Rottweiler Metzgerhund – the butcher's dog of Rottweil. There are many legends surrounding the breed. One says they came into Germany with the Roman legions, who used them as guard dogs and also to drive the herds of cattle needed to supply food for their advancing armies. Yet another suggests that they are descended from the strong, powerful boar-hunting dogs of the Swabian Knights. These dogs were put out to 'walk' as puppies, which is still done with Foxhound puppies in England. Severe penalties were inflicted on the 'puppy walkers' if the dogs were not returned in good condition, and it became the custom for the farmers to take them out with their own dogs when they were herding the cattle, so that they could keep an eye on them. As boarhunting decreased, fewer dogs were bred by the nobility and several were left on the farms. The farmers used them as guards and herders, and when the butchers came to buy their beasts often sold them the dogs to drive the cattle back to town.

The Rottweiler was imported from Germany to Britain in the 1930s and has increased in numbers ever since. Large powerful, thick-set dogs, they have smart black, smooth coats with tan markings and

Opposite page, top: Two attractive Maremma sheepdogs, from Italy.

Opposite page, bottom: Strong sensible guards, these two Rottweilers give the impression that they would soon see off any unwanted intruders.

Below: The Kuvasz is another newcomer to Britain and a relative of the Maremma and Pyrenean sheepdogs. It is a large dog and a keen guard which needs a sensible, capable owner.

intelligent brown eyes. They can still give a hand driving cattle if required, but nowadays Rottweilers are more likely to be seen giving a good account of themselves in working trials or on active duty with police forces.

The Giant Schnauzer, or the Riesenschnauzer as it is known in Germany, is another very old breed of herding dog which worked the cattle on the farms of southern Bavaria many years ago. Rather like the old-fashioned Kerry Blue from Ireland, the Schnauzer was expected to turn its hand to any job on the farm that a dog could do. It has plenty of initiative – too much for some owners – and can still do its original herding work, but today it is more often seen guarding docks and warehouses. Schnauzers have never really become very popular, although quite a few have spread

to Scandinavia. There is at least one working with the British police force, and making a good name for itself.

Schnauzers are large dogs, standing about 60 cm (2 ft), usually black or pepper and salt, and look what they are – tough, workmanlike dogs ready and willing to 'have a go', be it catching a criminal or bringing home the cattle.

Guard Dogs

ALTHOUGH the majority of present-day police and guard dogs come from the herding and allied breeds, there are a number which have always been bred as guard dogs. Most important of these are the various types of Mastiff, originally used as ferocious and fearsome war dogs.

Bas reliefs from Ancient Babylon, dated around 2000 BC, show dogs of Mastiff type going into battle with Hammurabi's armies. There are many other references to this type of dog being used by fighting armies right through the ages. Suits of armour worn by war dogs are to be seen in several European museums and there is one in the Tower of London.

History concentrates on two types of Mastiff: the Tibetan Mastiff and the Old English Mastiff. The Tibetan Mastiff has been described as the most savage dog in the world, but it has never established itself outside its native country and is now very rare even there. It is a huge, thick-coated dog, of similar type to several mountain dogs like the Pyrenean, Bernese and St Bernard.

The Old English Mastiff is much better known and its history is well documented for the past 2,000 years or so. When the Romans came to Britain, they were very impressed by these huge dogs which appear to have been quite numerous. An officer called the Procurator Cynegii was appointed the task of collecting and exporting Mastiffs to fight in the Roman arenas, where they were pitted against bears, lions and bulls, not to mention human beings. Later in its history, the Old English Mastiff was used in Britain as a guard dog to protect farms, castles and other property against human adversaries, and also to protect livestock from the attacks of wolves. Mastiffs were mentioned in the Forest Laws of King

Left: This Great Dane is showing a friendly interest in two orphan lambs.

Right: Not many people can afford to feed the large St Bernard today, or to keep one properly in modern towns and cities. .

Canute, and in Norman times they were the only breed, apart from the hounds belonging to the nobility, allowed in the forests, as long as they had their front claws cut off so that they could not hurt game.

The breed fought in the Battle of Agincourt and other wars of that period and was also used for the fashionable sports of bull- and bear-baiting. A Master of the King's Bears, Bulls and Mastiffs was created in the reign of Henry VIII, and in Elizabethan times plays were not allowed on Thursdays as that was the day reserved for bear-baiting. It was not until the early nineteenth century that animal baiting was banned in England and there immediately followed a great decline in the Mastiff population. Whether one agrees with a court ruling that baiting was a 'sweet and comfortable recreation for the solace and comforts of peaceable people', or with Samuel Pepys who described it as 'a very rude and nasty pleasure', it is sad to think that such a courageous animal, which held a unique position in the history of England for some 2,000 years, should suddenly become redundant.

There is no reason to suppose, because the Mastiff was used so much in the pursuit of a 'nasty pleasure', that it must be a nasty animal. On the contrary, dogs which are bold or even ferocious in the face of an adversary are usually most reliable with people, particularly children. Unlike the timid dog, they are not afraid of being hurt themselves and it is the nervous dog which is dangerous. Even in the days when the Mastiff was still being used in the bear pit and the bull ring, its virtues outside them appear to have been appreciated. At the beginning of the nineteenth century, Sydenham Edwards wrote in his *Cynographia Britannica*: 'What the lion is to the cat the Mastiff is to the dog, the noblest of the family; he stands alone and all others sink before him. His courage does not exceed his temper and generosity, and in attachment he equals the kindest of his race . . . In a family he will permit the children to play with him, and suffer all their little pranks without offence . . .'

In spite of their virtues, by 1908 only 35 Mastiffs were registered with the British Kennel Club. A few enthusiasts tried to preserve the breed, but keeping such a large dog going through two world wars was not easy. Only three litters were born in Britain between 1939 and 1945, and at the end of World War II only twenty Mastiffs remained in their native country,

most of them too old for breeding. Fortunately quite a number had been exported to America and the Old English Mastiff Club in Britain was able to buy some of these and take them back to England. This ensured the survival of the the breed on both sides of the Atlantic, although lack of fresh blood has proved quite a problem. Numerically the breed is still much stronger in America than in Britain and it is unlikely that it will ever rank amongst the top breeds in either country. On the other hand, the risk of extinction is now gone – for good, we hope – and British breeders are now exporting Mastiffs to many parts of the world.

Only one breed of dog has been specifically created in Britain as a guard dog, and that is the Bull Mastiff. It is very much a British product, being the result of crossing two of the oldest and purest of British breeds – the Bulldog and the Mastiff, remembering that the nineteenth-century Bulldog bore more resemblance to the Boxer of today than to the Bulldog, which would not survive in a bullring for more than a few minutes. The Bull Mastiff is one of the newest breeds and was not recognized by the British Kennel Club until 1924. But these dogs were used long before that by gamekeepers, who referred to them as 'night dogs' and used them to apprehend poachers. They were reputed to be trained to attack a man and throw him to the ground every time he tried to get to his feet, without ever using their teeth. There are records of contests and wagers over the ability of these dogs, one of which was reported in *The Field* of August 20, 1901:

Below: The handsome Bull Mastiff, a stalwart British guard dog breed.

Right: The Old English Mastiff.

Overleaf: Two handsome Boxers.

Opposite page, top: Not a pretty sight today, bear-baiting was a popular sport of the past.

Opposite page, bottom: A scene from the Medieval Bear and Boar Hunting Tapestry, showing huge mastiffs on the point of attacking a wild boar.

'Mr Burton of Thorneywood Kennels brought to the show one night dog (not for competition) and offered any person one pound who could escape from it while securely muzzled. One of the spectators who had had experience with dogs volunteered and amused a large assembly of sportsmen and keepers who had gathered there. The man was given a long start and the muzzled dog slipped after him. The animal caught him immediately and knocked him down with the first spring. The latter bravely tried to hold his own, but was floored every time he got to his feet, ultimately being kept to the ground until the owner of the dog released him. The man had three rounds with the powerful canine but was beaten each time and was unable to escape.'

The Bull Mastiff is still used by gamekeepers in Britain, and is one of the steadiest and most reliable of modern breeds. It makes a good, natural guard but is very reluctant to bite unless trained to do so. The very appearance of this dog, standing four square and staring a stranger straight in the eye, is enough to deter most people. Bull Mastiffs make quiet, stolid family dogs, reliable with children.

Although today not usually thought of as a guard dog, the Dalmatian has a long tradition in this field and was at one time also used as a war dog. There are various different theories about its origin, but it is known that years ago a dog very like the Dalmatian existed in Dalmatia on the eastern shores of the Gulf of Venice. These Dalmatian dogs did sentinel duty on the borders between Dalmatia and Croatia, to give warning against the inroads of invading Turks. Old engravings show

Dalmatians standing by chariots, and it appears that they have always had the strange affinity with horses for which they are so well known.

An American writer in 1901 said of the Dalmatian that 'now he is a dog of wheels and more connected with roads than inroads'. The breed has only fairly recently been upgraded to show dog and house pet, and for many years its place was in the stable yard, where it acted as a guard dog when not out with the carriages. Dalmatians were bred for stamina, and a newspaper report of 1851 tells of one dog which used to run with the Brighton to London coach – a distance of 116 km (72 miles). In the early part of the nineteenth century Dalmatians used to precede the carriages, but later they took up their station behind, the rear of the vehicle being quite unguarded.

Today Dalmatians are only usually seen out with carriages at horse shows. Apart from being very decorative, they make capable guards when left to look after an unattended vehicle.

As house pets, they are clean, short-haired dogs, not too large but with a tendency to shed white hairs. They need a lot of exercise and if left idle tend to get fat and bored. The pups are born white and the spots, liver or black, develop later.

The Great Dane, often known by many other names, has been around for centuries but the modern animal is essentially a fairly recent German product. The late Lord Rank called the breed 'gentlemanly, alert, courageous and elegant', an assessment many Great Dane owners would agree with.

The Great Dane looks, and is, an excellent guard dog. Its awe-inspiring appearance and deep-throated bark, almost a bay, should scare away all but the very bold or foolhardy.

Danes are not cheap to buy, rear or keep, but if you can afford one and have the facilities to keep it properly you will have a devoted companion and guardian. One problem that sometimes arises is its long tapered tail which can get in the way

indoors, knocking over furniture or people, and if confined for long the dog can do its tail a lot of damage.

The origin of the Boxer is not very clear, but it has only been known in its present form since the end of the nineteenth century. Quite likely it is a descendant of the old Bullenbeiser, which was once used in Germany for bull-baiting. When this cruel sport died out in Germany, the breed declined in numbers, but towards the end of the nineteenth century it received a boost of English Bulldog blood and finally emerged in 1895 at Munich as the Boxer. Since then the breed has never looked back and is well up in the popularity charts of most countries as a companion and guard dog.

Boxers are compact, short-coated, medium-sized dogs which soon caught the eye of the German police and were put into use with the Customs men and for general police duties. They are extremely boisterous dogs which take a long time to 'grow up', but they are ideal dogs for energetic owners.

The Doberman is a comparative newcomer and was created in the 1890s by Herr Doberman of Apolda. He used Rottweilers, German Pinschers, some varieties of Vorsthunde and maybe a dash of Weimaraner, the result being an elegant. streamlined dog, only too eager to go into action. Not surprisingly, the new breed inherited many of the tough working qualities of its ancestors and it was said of the earlier dogs that they feared nothing and that it took a brave man to own one. Their nature has softened in recent years but they still make formidable enemies, as many would-be criminals have discovered.

Dobermans are popular in the show ring and with police forces and armies all over the world, and Herr Doberman would be delighted to know that his skill and hard work have paid off so handsomely. The breed is well adapted to work in hot climates and is used with considerable success in the Middle East. In America many are used to guard stores and office blocks. They are well to the front in working trials and obedience classes and make exceptionally good tracking dogs. Kept as pets and companions they need careful handling and firm discipline, without bullying. A well-trained Doberman can make an excellent guard and companion; an untrained one can be a bit like carrying around a loaded gun – it may go off with disastrous results.

The term 'guard dog' tends to conjure up visions of large Alsatians chasing after desperate criminals or Dobermans ferociously guarding security vans, but many small breeds have served as guards for centuries and have done the job very well indeed.

The small, black, tailless Schipperke is one such guard dog. According to the archives of some Flemish towns, it was in use on the canal barges to repel boarders at least 150 years ago. Schipperkes were often to be seen riding on the tradesmen's vans, which they were left to guard while the vanmen made their deliveries. They are active, bustling, vigilant little dogs, and their shrill piercing bark gives obvious warning of strangers. Quite a number are shown in Britain, but not many are seen as pets. This is perhaps no bad thing as these active little dogs are not really suited to an idle life.

A larger breed, but still quite small compared with most guard dogs, is the Keeshond from Holland. At the beginning of the nineteenth century, most farms and barges had a Keeshond as a guard dog and they were used as such until about 1925 when they reached the show ring in several countries. Keeshonds make cheerful, adaptable companions and alert, sensible guards. They are medium-sized, do not eat a great deal nor take up a lot of room. Their grey, offstanding, thick coats look as though they would need a lot of grooming, but in fact water runs off the outer coat and mats seldom form. These dogs have plenty of personality and make good family dogs, usually only too happy to oblige the children with a game.

From the East comes the Lhasa Apso, usually associated with the monasteries where they were bred, although they were also owned by the ordinary people of Tibet. They are believed to be bringers of good luck and it is considered a great honour in Tibet to be given one as a present. Happy little dogs with thick coats, necessary in the Tibetan climate, they seem to have adapted to the Western world very well. They make courageous little guards and are quick to give warning.

Opposite page: This little Shih Tzu will have a lot more coat when it gets older.

Left: This Chow shows a very typical Oriental expression and also the black tongue. This is the only breed of dog which has the colour of its tongue mentioned in the breed standard.

Below: Strong, active and alert, this Doberman Pinscher looks capable of doing the job for which it was originally bred. The cropped ears would bar this dog from the show ring in Britain.

Also from Tibet comes the Lhasa Apso's larger cousin, the Tibetan Terrier, resembling a small Old English Sheepdog and in colours ranging from black to white. These dogs were often to be seen around the nomads' camps where they were expected to guard their master's property, including his children and livestock. Like the Lhasa Apso, they were also considered as a sort of talisman and good luck token. Another job they were expected to do was to retrieve objects which fell into awkward rocky places, which means that most of them have what is known as a good 'nose'. In summer they were often clipped with the sheep. and their thick hair was then mixed with Yak hair and woven into soft cloth. Quite a number are now shown and kept as companions. Most are charming little dogs. and they make discriminating guards.

Opposite page: It is easy to see why the Dalmatian got his nickname of 'Plum Pudding Dog'.

Above: Head study of a Bulldog.

Above: The Keeshund is a medium-sized Spitz breed from the Netherlands. A happy, sensible dog, but it does need to be kept well groomed.

Below: The Lhasa Apso is another breed that needs plenty of grooming.

Dogs in Miniature

TOY dogs? The very mention of them makes many people bristle, especially the owners of giant breeds. They conjure up visions of snuffling, yapping nuisances, of shivering Chihuahuas, of spoilt, bad-tempered Pugs slobbering all over their doting owner's laps. Not a very nice picture but fortunately a very wrong one. The dictionary defines the word 'toy' as a 'plaything, a trifling thing, not meant for real use'. So to call all the tiny dogs 'toys' is to do them a grave injustice. Many of these diminutive breeds pack more courage and intelligence into their small frames than some of the lumbering giants weighing 45 kg (100 lbs) or more.

Toy dogs are by no means a recent introduction. Many have been with us for centuries and it is worth first of all taking a look at some of these dogs from the past.

Probably the toy breed with the most ancient lineage is the Pekingese, or Lion Dog, of the Chinese Emperors. Dogs of very much the same type as the modern Pekingese can be identified from Korean bronzes dating back to 2000 BC. Their history was recorded by artists on scrolls now known collectively as the Imperial Dog Book. The Peke seems to have made its journey from East to West with its royal dignity untarnished, and still looks on other lesser breeds with great disdain. Incidentally, while the Pekingese is known as the Lion Dog of the East, the Maltese Terrier was in the past called the Lion Dog of the West.

Opposite page: A typical Pekingese attitude, surveying the world with disdain.

Below: Lion Dogs, the ancestors of the modern Pekingese, were bred to resemble dragons so that they would drive away evil spirits.

Below: Begging is an easy trick to teach a Pug – most have a good solid base to balance on!

Right: Two young King Charles Spaniel puppies.

Opposite page: Two dainty little Papillons.

Other toy breeds with a history behind them are the Toy Spaniel, famous for their connection with the Stuart King Charles II. These little dogs were often called 'Comforters' or 'Spaniels Gentle', probably because they were credited with special powers of healing if clasped to the bosom of a sick person. Toy Spaniels were firm favourites with many famous European artists long before they became accepted at the English Court.

The Papillon, or French Butterfly Dog, was also at one time called a toy spaniel. The name arises from the large, butterfly-shaped ears which are a feature of this breed. Oddly enough, they were at one time shown with drop ears, when it could hardly be said they resembled butterflies, or at best very sad ones. These little dogs were very popular as models for such painters as Rembrandt and Van Dyck.

Having seen how long many of the toy breeds have been in existence, one can refute the argument that they are very delicate and difficult to breed, although it must be said that some of the larger-headed, short-nosed breeds do have whelping troubles. So also do some of the scaled-down miniatures, such as the Toy Poodle, but chiefly because their ancestors were, until quite recently, possibly three times as large and throwbacks sometimes crop up. But taken all round, most toy dogs are tough, hardy little characters.

Soon after World War II people began to buy smaller dogs. Food was expensive and in short supply, and many people in towns lived in small houses with little opportunity to exercise a large dog. Toy

Charles and Cavalier King Charles Spaniels with their long silky coats and attractive colouring still retain their sporting instincts, and some are even used to work to the gun. They are cheerful, carefree little dogs, equally happy to share a city flat during the week or join you for a country ramble at weekends. Perhaps you will prefer the stolid Pug or quicksilver Chihuahua, both with nice easy-to-care-for coats. A quick rub over with a damp chamois leather and a final polish with your hands and these little dogs are neat and tidy, ready to take anywhere.

So take your pick from short coats, long coats, rough coats or fluffy coats, snub noses or almost no noses at all, medium noses and long pointed ones, small eyes or large eyes. Large protruding eyes must be

not have to go to such extremes with your own small house dog. It will not, of course, grow such a splendid coat as its brothers and sisters in the show ring but it will probably have a lot more fun in life. In fact, most toy dogs are very adaptable and, treated like dogs, not playthings, they are happy to go for a walk in the park, play ball in the garden or guard the car when you go shopping. (A word of warning about leaving dogs in cars, especially short-nosed breeds such as Pugs, Pekes and King Charles: even with the windows open, a car left in or out of the sun on a hot day can heat up to a very high temperature in a very short time.) As far as guarding is concerned, many of these tinies do a very good job indeed. They may not look as formidable as a German Shepherd, but the

dogs cost a great deal less to feed than a large breed, take up less room in a small house or car, cost less on public transport, need far less exercise and usually take less time to groom. But do not be misled into thinking that they cost less money to buy than a large dog. The opposite is probably true, one reason being that, while a larger breed may have ten to fifteen puppies in a litter, a bitch of the toy breeds will be more likely to produce four puppies at the most.

If you are thinking of buying a toy dog, the best place to see most of the breeds together is a large championship dog show. Dogs at shows are divided into groups to make it easier to judge them, and the group you will want to look out for will be the toy group. No matter what you are looking for in your small dog you should be able to find it here, all in miniature. The little King

treated with a little extra care if they are not to cause trouble. These eyes can pick up dust, cigarette ash or anything else floating around in the air, all of which will cause irritation. If it is only simple irritation the trouble can often be soothed by bathing the eye in a saline solution, 1 teaspoonful of salt to $\frac{1}{2}$ litre (1 pint) of water, making a solution very like the natural fluid of tears. Any serious scratch or blow to the eyes should be immediately referred to a veterinary surgeon.

If you are looking for a dog as a pet and companion rather than a show dog, do not be put off by all the preparation you see at dog shows. These dogs are entering what is really a canine beauty contest. The show Yorkie may well wear curlers every night and the Maltese be brushed and powdered to show off its profuse coat, but you will

noise they make will scare off any would-be car thief.

The pet toy dog will still need regular grooming, of course: brushing to keep its coat tangle-free, and a bath when necessary. What your little dog will also need is a thorough drying after being out in the wet, even if it is short-coated. The water itself will do it no harm while it is running about, but a small, low-to-ground dog will pick up an awful lot of moisture in a short time and must be well dried when it comes inside again. As good a way as any is to soak up the moisture with a chamois leather and give the dog a final rub with a rough towel; pat rather than rub dry if it has a very long coat.

Most dogs have small stomachs, and toy dogs especially should not be overfed. For the really tiny ones, two small meals a

Above: These attractive little long-haired Chihuahuas are sometimes confused with the Papillons shown on the previous page.

Opposite page: A proud King Charles Cavalier bitch with her litter of puppies.

day are often better than one large one. Some small dogs also have a tendency to develop bad teeth, possibly because their tiny mouths are pushed to the limit to accommodate the required number. You can help to remedy this by letting them have large raw bones to chew on and a hard dry dog biscuit occasionally. You should also check for tartar forming on the teeth, which will cause them to decay; if there does appear to be a thick deposit forming, then check with a veterinary surgeon. But most of the larger breeds have a few troubles too and, taken all round, a well-bred, well-reared and sensibly treated toy dog should be just as healthy and active as its bigger brothers.

One of the most popular toy breeds is the Toy Poodle. Small, chic, intelligent and a non-coat-shedder, it makes a good choice for the town flat. They first became popular

– indeed, almost over-popular – in the 1950s. This led to indiscriminate breeding by unscrupulous breeders and resulted in a great number of neurotic, nervous Poodles with slipping patellas, ingrowing eyelashes and many other unpleasant constructional faults. The popularity boom now seems to have worn off, however, and the Toy Poodles of today have greatly improved.

If you can manage to find a well-reared Toy Poodle puppy bred from sensible, healthy parents, you should have a pet to be proud of. They are usually jaunty, chic little chaps, willing and able to learn all sorts of tricks. Most Poodles have a very active brain as well as an agile body, and they have frequently been used in the circus to perform tricks. They seem to appreciate an audience and the more you teach them, the more they enjoy it. Their small size is no bar to working them in obedience classes

and quite a few have made a name for themselves in this sort of work. So if you want your Poodle to be a happy little dog, let it use its brain and give it plenty to do. If you treat it like a lapdog and fuss over it, it will probably develop into a neurotic little horror, but you will only have yourself to blame.

Poodles have the advantage over other breeds in that they do not shed their coats, but on the other hand they do need careful and regular grooming and clipping. They have a tendency to grow excess hair in the entrance to the ear canal, and this must be regularly plucked out or it will get matted and block the ear, causing endless trouble. If you start when the dog is a puppy and gently pluck out the hair with forefinger and thumb, it should never get to the stage where it causes trouble. White poodles also tend to get 'tear marks' below the eyes. These cause little harm but they look most unattractive. The eyes can be bathed in a saline solution or even cold tea, and there are special preparations on sale at good pet stores which are most effective. Always check to see that the dog has not got ingrowing eyelashes which are causing this trouble; if so take it to your veterinary surgeon.

Poodles can be professionally clipped at beauty salons, or you can learn to do it yourself if you simply want a smart pet. In either case, the earlier clipping is started the better. Treated firmly but gently as a puppy, the dog will soon accept clipping as part of its general routine and will even look forward to it.

If you decide to clip the dog yourself, have a look round the poodle benches at dog shows and chat to the exhibitors. Buy an illustrated book on the art of clipping and make a start with a good pair of electric clippers. Always be very light-handed; most cases of 'clipper rash' and of dogs disliking clipping are due to a heavy-handed clipper. Should a rash develop, dab baby lotion or cream over the affected part and dust with talcum powder. Be very careful clipping the tail for the first time; it is very sensitive and if you have the clippers adjusted too finely you can cause the dog a lot of pain and irritation.

You can start clipping when the puppy is about eight weeks old. All that is necessary at this stage is to clip the feet, face and tail. As the coat gets longer, it will need 'tipping' slightly with scissors to keep it even. If you only intend to keep the pup as a pet and not for showing, it is best to shape the topknot into a neat round. Puppy hair is very soft and breaks easily, so do not leave ribbons or rubber bands on for very long. Never do too much at once; far better to clip two feet and then let the puppy have a rest, than subject it to a long session. Be extra careful when the pup is teething at about the age of five months; it is best not to clip round its face at all for a while as its mouth might be sore.

The two most popular pet clips are the Dutch, or Cowboy, and the Lamb. The Lamb is the most practical, consisting of short curls all over with feet, face and tail clipped. In the Dutch Clip the feet, face, tail and body are all clipped, leaving a pompom on the tail, a rounded topknot and big baggy trousers. Sometimes a moustache is left on but this is simply a matter of choice.

If you give the dog a bath before clipping, you will get a better finish. And remember that even if your poodle is clipped regularly, it will still need grooming.

The Japanese Chin, or Japanese Spaniel as it was once known, came from Japan in about 1882. The breed caught the public's fancy and soon a considerable number were being imported and exhibited at dog shows. They soon became a great favourite with Queen Victoria and she had her portrait painted with one. Although fairly new to the Western world, the breed has existed in the East for centuries. No one seems to know its exact origin, but it is thought that it had as ancestors the Pekingese and a now extinct feathered variety of Pug called the Loong Chua.

Weighing about 3 kg (7 lbs), the Japanese Chin is a very smart little dog, black and white or red and white, marked in distinct patches. Its coat is long and straight, with a pronounced ruff and feathering on the legs and feet. The tail is well plumed and carried proudly over the back. Slightly higher on the leg than the better-known Pekingese, the Japanese is noted for its energy and love of life. Its gait is high-stepping and graceful. It enjoys jumping and both you and your pet will get a lot of fun from some small 'hurdles' put up in the garden.

Japanese Chins are usually good house dogs. They have a deep bark for their small size, but they are not usually 'yappers', like some other tinies. Most owners of Japs find they are very good mixers and get on well with dogs of other breeds. As the standard calls for rather prominent eyes, particular care should be taken to keep these clean and free from dust and grit, if necessary washing them with saline solution (see above). Their silky coats should be kept in

Opposite page, left: This Poodle in a pet trim is obviously enjoying his country outing.

Opposite page, right: A well-balanced little Toy Terrier.

Right: A large and lively family of Japanese Chins.

good condition by brushing; use a wide-toothed comb if the dog is shedding its coat or has got some tangles, but don't overdo the comb work as it will tend to pull out too much coat. Make sure there are no mats between the toes or behind the ears, and always keep the feathering on the hindquarters particularly clean.

When the dog is casting its coat, a bath can be a help in loosening the dead undercoat and giving the new one a better chance to grow through. Use a towel to sop up the surplus water, then use a hairdryer and gently brush the dog dry at the same time. This way the coat will not get broken and will lie much flatter.

Japs are intelligent little dogs and, like all dogs, are the better for some training. It gives them a chance to use their brains and makes for a better and closer relationship between dog and owner.

The English Toy Terrier has had quite a few different names in the last century, including Toy Manchester Terrier, Toy Black and Tan, and Miniature Black and Tan, but English Toy Terrier seems to be the final choice. It is a very old British breed, and many years ago a great deal of money was won and lost on these little terriers in the rat pits where their record stood second to none.

Toy Terriers make delightful house dogs, especially for the smaller house or flat. Most are undemanding little dogs, but they are very keen and alert and will soon give warning if strangers are about. Although quite small, the ideal weight being between 2.7–3.6 kg (6–8 lbs) in Britain and up to 5.4 kg (12 lbs) in America, they still retain their sporting instincts and remain real terriers. Sturdy as well as elegant to look at, most would still welcome the chance to have a go at a rat, or even a mouse.

These miniature terriers have a sleek, glossy coat and longish legs which keep them well up out of the dirt, so they need the minimum of time and trouble spent to keep them looking well groomed. All that is necessary is a good brushing with a short, stiff brush or glove, a wipe with a damp chamois leather and a final polish with your hands to give a good gloss. In colouring, they are a clearly defined pattern of jet black and rich mahogany tan. The colours must never run into each other, but

should appear quite separate. The head is black with two tan cheek spots, tan spots over each eye and a tan muzzle. The legs from the knee down are tan, but the toes are pencilled in black. No white is allowed. They have fairly large upright ears, and stand about 28 cm (11 ins) high, making a smart, distinctive little dog.

Another good point in the Toy Terriers' favour is that they are not usually fussy feeders and have small appetites. They are not shivery little dogs but, only having very short coats, they do tend to feel the cold and wet. If kept on the move they will enjoy a run in bad weather, but they should not be allowed to stand around and should be well dried on return. A warm comfortable bed will also be appreciated and this could be combined with a small travelling box, lined with a warm blanket.

The smallest breed of dog in the world, and one of the most popular, is the Chihuahua. The standard states their weight as being under 2.7 kg (6 lbs) and even more diminutive is preferred. Unhappily, although they usually weigh 1.8–2.7 kg (4–6 lbs), some have been recorded weighing as little as 450 gm (1 lb). If you shrink a breed to a third of its size or less in a few generations, you are almost bound to breed trouble. Some of these very small Chihuahuas have a considerable amount of hip trouble and the bitches often have very difficult whelpings, requiring caesarean operations to enable them to have their litters. So should you decide on one of these fascinating small dogs, try to find a slightly larger one and you will find it a lot easier to manage.

It is generally accepted that these little

dogs originated in Mexico in the state of Chihuahua, from which they take their name. The first one was registered with the American Kennel Club in 1904. Chihuahuas still exist in their original form, slightly larger and tougher than the pet dog we know, in Indian villages in Central America. Travellers have brought back tales of packs of fifty or more enthusiastically hunting wild pigs in the forests! I doubt if the show dogs would appreciate that pastime, but they are still agile, alert little dogs, usually very intelligent and devoted to their owners but none too keen on strangers. This is not a bad thing as it generally makes them good house dogs and less likely to be stolen.

If you do not like the short-coated Chihuahua, there is also a long-coated variety. The standard is the same for both types except that the longer coat should be soft, often with a slight wave. The tail is well plumed and the feet and legs are well feathered. The ears are fringed and there should be a large ruff round the neck. As with the smooth variety, any colour or combination of colours is permissible. The smooths may feel the cold a bit and some appreciate a warm polo-necked sweater on a cold winter's day, but their coats take very little looking after to keep them soft and shining. A good daily massage with the hands and a brisk rub with a damp chamois leather to remove dirt and loose hairs are about all you need to do. The long-coated Chihuahuas are also easily kept in good condition by a short daily session with brush and comb. Their teeth need watching carefully as their mouths are very small and the teeth may be a bit cramped, so try to get

the dog used to having its mouth handled while it is still a puppy. Brush the teeth with a toothbrush and scale them if necessary, thus avoiding any build-up of tartar. The dog's nails also need an eye kept on them and should not be allowed to grow too long.

Yet another smart, smooth-coated tiny is the Miniature Pinscher. Usually black and tan, red or chocolate in colour, it makes a lively companion. Although often described as a small edition of the Doberman Pinscher, this is not correct. Min Pins were in existence long before Herr Doberman introduced his namesake to the dog world. A rather different toy breed is the rough-coated Griffon, which with its quaint monkey face has a charm all its own.

A newcomer to the West is the pretty little Bichon Frise, a small white dog with a double coat, the outer hair long and silky. Its ears are sometimes tinged with cream, apricot or grey. These little dogs have a lot of character and are very lively.

Above left: Three smart Miniature Poodles in a 'lion clip', the usual trim used for showing.

Right: A young Bichon Frise pup ready for a game.

Overleaf: One advantage of small dogs like this Yorkshire Terrier is that you don't need to buy a dog bed – you can keep it in your hat!

Overleaf, inset: A giant Dogue de Bordeaux shows up the size of this tiny Chihuahua.

Dogs on Show

FOR years the rat pit, the dog pit, the bear pit and the bull ring provided an opportunity for men to test their skill at producing dogs to beat the dogs belonging to other people. These were hard men who lived in hard times and we must excuse them if they appear to have had little feeling for the suffering of dumb animals. In the early nineteenth century dog fighting and the baiting of other animals were made illegal, and so, instead, some owners started matching their dogs against each other for appearance only. With the development of dog shows came an entirely new 'breed' of dog owner.

The first record of an organized dog show was at Newcastle-on-Tyne in June 1859, when there was one class for setters and one for pointers. In 1873 the British Kennel Club was founded and has been recognized as the ruling body in Britain ever since. Over 3,500 shows are held under Kennel Club rules every year in Britain, as well as about 300 field and working trials. All dogs shown at recognized shows, which means practically all dog shows in Britain, must be registered at the Kennel Club, and the same applied to field trials for gun dogs, working trials for police dogs and obedience classes. It does not, however, apply to sheepdog trials, which are held under the rules of the International Sheepdog Society; hound shows, which are run by the Masters of Foxhounds Association; and coursing matches, which are held under the rules of the National Coursing Club.

As the cult of showing dogs has spread throughout the world, governing bodies have been founded in each country to see fair play. Anyone contemplating showing a dog should contact their own Kennel Club to find out what shows are available and what rules and regulations must be adhered to.

Left: Small dogs like this Yorkshire Terrier are usually judged standing on a table.

Right: Preparations such as these are necessary if a Yorkshire Terrier is to look like the prizewinner opposite.

The merit of dog shows has often been queried and opposing factions believe that many breeds have been either improved or ruined as a result of showing. Nevertheless, many breeds, such as the Irish Wolfhound and the Old English Mastiff, would be extinct if it were not for dog shows. And it is the people who exhibit dogs who breed the thousands of pure-bred puppies necessary to supply the pet market. Although there are also thousands of mongrel puppies which can be purchased much more cheaply, one has no idea what a mongrel puppy will turn out to be like; with a pure-bred puppy, one at least has a fair idea of what it will look like when grown up and what sort of characteristics it is likely to develop. For choosing the sort of dog you would like, dog shows are the best place to see a wide variety of breeds.

For people who criticize the whole idea of showing animals, it is difficult to explain the attraction. It is certainly not done for the money and very few people have ever made money by showing dogs. A lot of satisfaction is to be derived from producing an animal to such a high standard that it beats all the others in its class. To win best of breed or, better still, best in show at a championship show is a very real thrill and one experienced by comparatively few people. To those interested in genetics, the breeding of any animal to certain high standards of perfection is a never-ending source of pleasure and satisfaction.

Dog shows in Britain are graded from championship shows at the top through open shows down to matches and exemption shows. The classes at the shows are graded from open down to novice, with titles like

123

postgraduate and mid-limit to make it all very confusing for the uninitiated. The important point to remember is that when the dog has won a certain number of the lower classes at the lower shows, it can then only enter into the higher classes. If it eventually becomes a champion, it can only compete in open classes at championship and open shows. To become a champion in Britain, a dog must win three challenge certificates under three different judges, each of whom must sign a declaration saying that in their opinion the dog is 'clearly worthy of the title of champion', and these titles can only be won at championship shows which are chosen by the Kennel Club. In America, Canada and most other countries the principles are the same although the methods of carrying them out may be different.

To anyone with an inclination to take up pedigree dog breeding as a hobby or who feels like showing the dog they already have, the first advice is to go along to several shows and try to find out what it is all about. Go to one or two big championship shows, but also take a look at your local show because that is where you should start showing. Watch how the experts handle their dogs and don't forget that today's experts were yesterday's novices.

When you go to dog shows you will hear all sorts of stories about judges who 'judge the other end of the lead'. This is often the complaint of the owner who shows a dog unsuccessfully for quite a long time, then sells it to another owner who immediately starts winning with it. He has overlooked the fact that the second owner

is obviously an expert who has presented the dog to such perfection that it hardly resembles the dog dragged round the shows for so long by its previous owner. Presentation and showmanship won't turn a bad dog into a good one, but it can make it look a great deal better.

The dog's appearance depends a great deal on what has been done before the show. With so much difference between the various breeds, there must obviously be equally great differences in preparation. 'Breed books' devoted to each breed often give detailed advice on how to prepare that particular breed for the show ring, and experienced exhibitors are usually very pleased to help a novice. Nevertheless, there are several general points worth mentioning. Good condition, as we have already seen, 'goes in at the mouth'. No amount of grooming or trimming can make up for good health provided by good food and adequate exercise. I use the word 'adequate' deliberately; one does not want to get a show dog as fit and hard as, say, a racing Greyhound. The show dog should, in fact, carry more flesh to give a rather more rounded appearance.

To win in the show ring a dog must walk properly on a lead, stand to be handled by the judge and have a general air of self-possession. To do so it must have confidence in its handler, who cannot inspire such confidence if he or she is a bundle of nerves. This explains why a professional handler can often get more out of a dog he has never seen before than the owner, who knows it well. The advice given earlier on socializing puppies applies just as much to show dogs as to dogs kept as pets. It is important to take the dog out as a puppy to meet other dogs. Training classes can be a help and some canine societies run handling classes

Opposite page: Foxhounds have their own recognized shows, where, unlike most dog shows, the hounds are judged loose and not on a lead.

Above: This long-coated Chihuahua looks justly proud of the huge cups it has won at Crufts Dog Show.

Above right: Canine beauticians carrying their art to extremes, to prepare a dog for a special occasion.

Top: The line-up at Crufts, perhaps the best-known dog show in the world – but this class of Pyreneans seems to find it all rather a bore.

for 'beauty' dogs, as opposed to 'obedience' dogs.

Confusion is often created in the minds of newcomers to dog showing because the judge at one show will often reverse the placings of a judge at another show. Judging is done according to a standard of points laid down for each and every breed, but although the standard is always the same different judges interpret it in different ways. One judge's idea of what is 'moderately wide between the ears' may be very different from another's. It is a good thing, maybe, that judges do differ; if everyone could agree on the perfect dog, then that dog would win all the prizes and there would be no point in anyone else showing! Experienced exhibitors learn to know which judges like their type of dog and try to show under these. Big breeders will often show one dog under one judge and a different dog under another, but even

then they are not assured of automatic success.

Many people put their dog or dogs in the hands of a professional handler, who prepares and shows it for them. They then go along to see it win (or lose), rather like a racehorse owner goes to the races. To me half the fun of showing is in preparing and handling the animal oneself. Nevertheless professional handling is very common in America and for some breeds in Britain. Practically all Wire Fox Terriers and several other terriers are handled by professionals. It must be admitted that it is very difficult for a novice to win in these breeds against the experts, but amateurs do still win against the professionals and the satisfaction of doing so is even greater than when one wins against other amateurs.

Below: The hustle and bustle of the Airedale ring at Crufts.

Index

Figures in italics refer to illustrations

Acknowledgments

The publishers would like to thank the following individuals and organizations for their kind permission to reproduce the photographs in this book:

A.F.I.P.: 4, 120–121, (A. M. Berenger) 8, (Gerard Mathieu) 35 left; Ardea: (Jean-Paul Ferrero) 1, 61 above, 74 above, 82–83, 121 inset; Australian News and Information Bureau: 91; Bavaria Verlag: 107 above; S. C. Bisserot: 70 above, 110; Camera and Pen International: (C. de Jaeger) 16 left, (Max Wilkins) 52 right; Bruce Coleman: (Hans Reinhard) 2–3, 33, 34 above, 35 right, 90, 96, 99 below, (J. van Wormer) 12; Bruce Coleman Inc.: (Leonard Lee Rue III) 83 above; Gerry Cranham: 30, 125 above; Anne Cumbers: 49, 55, 68 below, 76, 97, 98 below, 117, 122, 123; Daily Telegraph: (John Sims) 19; Gary Ede: 116 left; Mary Evans Picture Library: 103 above; Will Green: 47; Sonia Halliday: 9; Robert Hallmann: 101; Michael Holford: 50 above, 103 below, 111; Jacana Agence de Presse: (B. Josedupont) 94–95, 109 left, (J. H. Labat) 37, (Nadeau) 61 below, (P. Pilloud) 58 above, (B. Rebouleau) 73, (Soyamoto) 81, 119, (G. Trouillet) 93, 113; Paolo Koch: 125 centre right; Frank H. Meads: 52 left; Jim Meads: 40–41, 41, 42–43, 44, 45, 46, 48–9; Metropolitan Police: 92 below; John Moss: 34 below, 68 above, 79 above, 87, 95 above, 106; Daniel O'Keefe: 70 below left; Mike Peters: 51; Pictor: 56–57, 75, 85 below, 108, 114, 115, (Alpha) 83 below, (Tony Frissell) 14–15; Dick Polak: 18, 20, 21, 23 above left, 23 below left, 23 below centre, 23 right, 26 below right, 26 above left and right, 27, 28; Popperfoto: 29; John Rigby: 80; Spectrum: 10 below, 32 above, 50 below, 60, 67 below, 104–105, 124, 128; John Massey Stewart: 31; Tony Stone Assoc., endpapers; Syndication International: 126; Sally Anne Thompson: 10 above, 11 above and below, 16 right, 17, 22, 24, 25, 26 below left, 36, 38–39, 53 left, 54, 59, 62, 63, 64, 65 below, 66, 67 above, 69, 70 below right, 71, 72, 74 below, 77 above, 78, 79 below, 85 above, 86, 88, 89 right, 98 above, 102 above and below, 107 below, 109 right, 112 left, 112 right, 116 right, 118, 125 centre left; Tiofoto: 83 centre; Elizabeth Weiland: 32 below, 58 centre, 58 below, 65 above, 84, 89 left; Barbara Woodhouse: 6–7, 77 below, 100; ZEFA: 53 right, 92 above, (W. Schmidt) 13.